Love Made in Heaven

Secrets to an Amazing Life, Relationship and Marriage

by Marielle McCormick
with Del McCormick

Revelation Press

Love Made in Heaven: Secrets to an Amazing
Life, Relationship and Marriage
Copyright @ 2013 by Marielle and Derek
McCormick
Edited by Danette Pelletier

Published by Revelation Press
Printed in the United States of America

Scripture quotations are taken from the Holy
Bible, New Living Translation, Copyright @
1996, Tyndale House Foundation. Used by
permission of Tyndale House Publishers, Inc.,
Carol Stream, Illinois 60188

To my beloved husband Del,

Thank you for your input on this project. This book would not exist without you. If I had one wish, it would be to go back over 28 years to the day we first met and relive those years with you all over again. It has been more fun than I could have ever imagined.

This book is dedicated to our awesome children – Colin, Liam, and Tayler, our new kids, Sam and Melissa, and our little grandson, Christian.

Special thanks to our son-in-law, Sam, who kept telling me to find a way to teach others how to have a great marriage. I had no idea where that would lead.

Thanks to my mother, Josie, Aunt Nan, and especially Uncle Rick, who taught me at an early age the wonderful joy of telling a funny story.

Our lives have been wonderful, thanks to my mother, our children, my sister Liz, my brother Diego and his wife Heidi, my husband's brother, Colin, their parents Cathy and Derek, my aunts and uncles, my always-fun cousins, my special nieces and nephews, and all of our large extended family.

We also remember Del's family and friends in the UK and all of our great friends from childhood to present. You have all played a huge role in making our lives fun!

Table of Contents

Why Dating Works 6

Respect and Communication...................................23

Appearance – Working with What You Have 38

Beneficial Friendships and Dealing with the Past...51

Fighting Constructively 70

Managing Finances 85

Roles and Responsibilities.....................................103

Secrets and Lies 116

Date Nights, Snuggling and Intimacy.....................125

Drifting Apart..138

Left for Last: The Best-Kept Secret 148

Chapter 1
Why Dating Works

Oh, to be young and in love, as the old saying goes. The magic of your heart racing, when you see that person you like walk by. You're nervous and shaking when they approach to possibly acknowledge you. They say your name, and you think you are going to die. They remembered your name and actually know who you are. You cannot believe it. You think of nothing but that person you like, day and night.

I remember it began in about the fifth grade. I was at a summer neighborhood music festival. Some young boys, about 12 or 13 years old, were playing on one of the stages in a band. I noticed the young drummer right away. He was having so much fun, tossing his hair around as he played. He was so enjoying his music. I was mesmerized by this young boy.

I found out that he lived just a few blocks away. He practiced his drums every day in his room, next to a window that faced the street. I rode my bike by that house nearly every day just to sneak a peek at him practicing his drums. This went on for nearly two years.

In seventh grade, I started junior high. He was a student there and about two years older than me. One day, I was across the street from our school outside a local dime store. I noticed him approaching with a girl by his side. Suddenly, he said hello to me and said my name. I thought, "Oh my gosh, he knows my name!"

Time stopped for me that day. I think that was one of the happiest days of my life up until then. Nothing ever came of that relationship, but I still have a picture of him in front of his house, one that I took one day when I rode by on my bike. It's in a box somewhere in my garage to this day.

Go back and remember your thoughts at that age. You'd ask your friends what you could do to get that special person to like you more. When they started to notice you and give you some extra attention, you were flying on a cloud. One wink in your direction was enough to make you melt. If they touched your hand, you didn't want to wash it. When they put their arms around you, you wanted to stay like that forever. That first kiss made your heart flutter with happiness. When you became a couple, you wanted everyone to know it.

LOVE IS IN THE AIR, AND NOTHING ELSE MATTERS

Being young and in love is amazing. When you start dating someone that you're crazy about, everything is fun, exciting, and amazing, full of life and *on fire*. You've never met anyone this great, and they can do no wrong. Everything they say is perfect. Everything they *do* is wonderful. They are just so good looking. No one has *ever* looked this good. Sometimes, they say something dumb, but you think it's cute. Your friends think your sweetie's just *okay*, but you're convinced they just don't see what you see. You don't have much in common, but you will kill yourself to make it work with them.

Remember that boy or girl in school you were crazy about? Were they perfect? In reality, no, they weren't. In your eyes, you didn't notice that their clothes didn't really match. Instead, you loved their unique look. Their hair was a little messy, but you thought it was super-stylish. They weren't very bright, but you thought they were so funny, so smart.

If a guy showed up at my door in ripped-up jeans, I remember thinking, "I *love* that style!" Your new honey's family might be a bit different, but you like them, anyway. He rides a bike or drives a beat-up car, but you'd go with him anywhere. He isn't the best student, but to you, he's a genius. He doesn't have the best job, but you know he has the potential to go far in whatever he does. Do you remember thinking that way when you were young and in love? Maybe you're experiencing this right now and know what I'm talking about.

And this phenomenon doesn't only apply to women. Men will also overlook things about the girls they like. If they're late, that's fine. If they're too chatty or too quiet, that doesn't matter, either. No matter what the issue may be, they'll let it slide – as long as they think the girl is really cute!

For me, the dating years were great fun. In high school, my girlfriends and I had crushes on lots of young boys. We got together in groups of guys and girls who kind of liked each other. We'd ride around together in a big, old convertible that belonged to my girlfriend's father. We'd always squeeze at least ten kids into the car.

We had such fun riding around town in the evenings with the top down and the wind blowing our hair, even in the winter, when it was chilly outside. It doesn't get very cold in Florida where I went to high school, but it was still cold riding around in that car with the top down. We used to bring a huge blanket to cover all of us as she drove around. We'd be underneath it, laughing and giggling, because it filled with air like we were in a big tent. Sometimes, we'd throw the blanket over her head for a minute while she was driving and she'd scream. We wanted the boys to think we were so much fun.

Some evenings, we'd go to the drive-in movies with our group of friends. I think most teens from that era would agree that the drive-in theater was probably the best invention ever.

Sometimes, we'd sit under the moonlight outside on a blanket or in the car, while trying to get the boys we liked to really notice us.

There just seemed to be cute boys everywhere at that age. It was like having eye candy everywhere you went. I remember being obsessed with a few boys. I pretty much had the best job in high school and college. I worked at a candy kiosk in the middle of the mall. I was surrounded by chocolate every day, and I still think that was my favorite job I ever had. I also had a view from every angle of the boys walking through the mall. Sometimes, if they were really cute, I'd blow them a kiss as they walked by.

My girlfriends and I were all boy-crazy, so crazy, in fact, that we once spent an entire evening lying in a boy's front yard, hiding in the grass so we could spy on this boy that my girlfriend liked. We watched for hours to see if any other girls came by. Of course, we could see him, but he never knew how desperate we were to see what he was doing.

During those days, my friends and I also used to sneak into the boys' dorm at the local university and pretend we were students there to try to get dates with college boys. Soon, my girlfriends and I started dating the ones we liked. Everything was all about the guys. We'd put a lot of thought into how to treat them, how to surprise them with fun nights out or spoil them with thoughtful gifts, and they'd do the same for us. I remember roses sitting on my dresser for months. Yes, they were dried-up, black, and falling apart, but I didn't want to throw them away – ever.

We fussed over these boys as often as we could. All of our thoughts centered on how to make them happy or make them fall for us. It didn't matter what it took. We were determined to do it. Love was in the air, and nothing else mattered.

MY LOVE IS AMAZING, PERFECT, INCREDIBLE...

Why does dating work? Why are these early stages of dating so incredible? Because you're totally focused on the other person and not yourself. And he's focused on you!

You ask yourself, "What does he like to do? I'll arrange it. Where does he like to eat? I'll take him to his favorite restaurant instead of mine. I'll go see that action movie he's dying to see, even though I'd prefer a romantic movie. What concert would he enjoy the most? I haven't listened to country music, but I'll give it a try. Who would he like to hang out with? I'll go out with his friends, even though I don't really know them."

Your total aim is to please the person you like. You dress in your best clothes. You're not just throwing on an old tee shirt. You're not content to put your hair up in a quick ponytail. No, you spend time carefully fixing it. You don't just wash your face. Instead, you carefully apply your makeup. You don't just say whatever's on your mind. You're careful of every word you say.

THE FOCUS STARTS TO SHIFT

Why do most relationships get boring after a while? Because you stop doing all of these things. Your focus has shifted. What has it shifted to? None other than yourself. Society teaches us that you're Number One.

It asks, "Are you satisfied?" Are you getting what you deserve? Do you live in the house you've always wanted? Do you have the car you really want? Do you have the relationship you deserve? Are you as wealthy as you should be?"

Okay, I just used the word "you" thirteen times! Do you see the problem? You no longer view your mate as the most important person in your life.

Your focus has changed. Your attention used to be on him, but now you're so concerned with yourself that you don't worry about your love anymore.

Your sweetheart wants to go to a game. But instead of going and keeping him company, you complain that you don't like sports. Back in the day, you would have gone! Your honey wants to go fishing, but instead of spending the day lying in the sun with your love, you reply, "No thanks."

Remember when you were dating? You went to ball games, movies, and concerts. Just hanging out was fun. You were willing to do anything together. You didn't focus on yourself during that time. Your love also returned that focus, because you were spoiling him, and he liked being fussed over.

What's most important to your mate? That you make them feel like they are the most important person in the world to you, that no one is better, and no one ever will be. In the early days, you didn't have to try. Your attention was automatically on him. It all seemed so easy and wonderful.

When I was young, I always liked the fun, mischievous boys. I was drawn to their free spirit and playfulness. At the grade school I attended in Wisconsin, there were a couple of boys I'd known since kindergarten. They were always getting into harmless trouble. They seemed to make our school days so much fun. They broke up the boredom of learning stuff we didn't really care about.

One day in the sixth grade, one of those boys got in trouble and was sent to sit out in the hallway for doing something silly. It has been a while, but as I remember it, I was sent out to the hallway as well. We had to sit there as punishment.

Outside the classroom, above a long bench, hung hooks on which to place our coats during those freezing Wisconsin winters. Above the coats was a long shelf that held our hats and gloves. There were several windows above the shelf where you could look down into the classroom. That day, my friend thought it would be fun to take all of the gloves and line them up in a long row along the windows with the middle finger of each glove extended, one after another, for all of our classmates to see.

We really didn't know what that gesture meant, but we knew it was something naughty. Everyone was laughing, but the teacher didn't know why. Oh, I had so much fun that day with that boy and many other times after that. Even though I live in Florida now, we've kept in touch over the years and remain friends.

Everyone really wants to be in a relationship that's playful like the relationships of our youth in order to offset the stresses of adult life. As my girlfriend has explained to her young son, "Don't be in such a hurry to grow up. Being a kid is so much fun! Being an adult *blows!*" Well, I don't totally agree with that sentiment, but it's funny, and I understand what she really means.

When you're young, you get to enjoy yourself with very little responsibility. In high school, you get to hang out with your friends, cheer on your school team, join clubs, act in a play, sing or join the school band. In college, you attend parties on Friday and Saturday nights. You can nap under a tree on the campus in the afternoon. The library is for studying or spying on some cute guy you've noticed.

Test coming up? No problem. You'll cram all night the day before. You wonder who's dating who. Do you have a chance getting a date with so-and-so? Remember thinking those things? The only responsibility you have is waking up and getting somewhere and trying to halfway do most things. So easy to do, and so much time left over to have lots of fun. Can you stay this age forever? The answer for most is going to be, sorry, but no.

TIME CONTINUES, AND WE HAVE TO GROW UP

Now, some years have passed. You've become an adult, and your thoughts have gotten serious. You're worried about paying the bills on time. How do you keep the house clean? Will your car make it to your job today? Why can't the kids get themselves up in the morning? Why doesn't your spouse help out more around the house? You may feel tired now. Cooking is not so much fun, day after day. You've got to buy food and clothes, pay the mortgage. What happened? You grew up!

You became that person you said you could never relate to. You've become like Mom and Dad. Life as an adult is hard, with a lot of responsibility, but if you have a relationship that's playful most of the time, it makes things a lot easier.

Don't be discouraged at the thought of entering adulthood. Here's a little secret. Who says you have to be totally grown up when you become an adult? Does it hurt anyone if you still enjoy the kid inside of you once in a while? No, it doesn't.

Do you laugh the way you did when you were a kid? Do you watch a funny show on TV regularly, or are you focused on watching the disasters on the news? Do you go and enjoy a light movie here and there, or do you fall asleep in the recliner each night?

Do you take a day to treat yourself and your honey to a nice restaurant for lunch, or do you go through the drive-thru and coat your arteries with some fast food?

RETURNING TO WHAT WORKS

The point is, you must consciously focus on how you kept your relationship going the way you did when you were young and continue using those methods. If you want to keep your relationship fun and exciting long-term, you can never stop doing those things. Things that work don't really change. Being young at heart has a greater meaning than we think. It means keeping your actions soft and thoughtful. Walking confidently, but playfully seeing things not just through your own eyes, but through your mate's as well.

Even as you get older and life gets more complicated, you can still have just as much fun as the kid who made everyone laugh while you were growing up. Remember that kid? Everyone wanted to be around that boy or girl. Who doesn't want to be around someone that's having fun? I promise your mate does. Never stop dating. It doesn't matter if you've been together one year or ten. Go out to dinner. Go to the beach. See a movie. Hold hands. Walk through a park together. The key is to keep the days of your youth alive!

Chapter 2
Respect and Communication

Do you still respect your mate? In the beginning of your relationship, they could do no wrong. If they said something silly, you laughed. If they were confused, you tried to help them understand. If they got upset, you tried to calm them down.

When your relationship is new, you have so much respect for your new love that you treat them better than everyone else. Your words are soft and encouraging. Your perception of what they say is so clear, because you're so focused on every word they say. They have your full attention.

Everyone wants to feel respected and know that what they have to say is important. In the beginning, you agree on decisions together. You ask your mate's opinion before you make that final choice. You put their opinions before your own, because in the beginning, getting your own way is not nearly as important as encouraging your sweetheart.

Men need to feel that you respect them. This is more important to them than anything. Women need to feel loved. When I first met my husband, he was new to this country. Having grown up in London, he still had a strong British accent. When we were first dating, I really couldn't understand much of what he said. I'd listen intently when he spoke, with stars in my eyes, before saying, "I don't know what you're saying, but it sounds really cool."

New couples often put their own individual needs to the side, preferring to focus on their mate and what pleases them. I remember listening to new music that my husband liked and trying new foods at unfamiliar restaurants I wouldn't normally think of trying. I accepted his friends, even though I didn't have much in common with some of them. Eventually, his friends became important to me, as well. When you're focused on making your relationship work, you accept many differences and work at getting along.

When you first met your mate, what activities did you enjoy together? My husband and I both loved music. He'd grown up listening to music from the sixties and seventies and fondly remembered the music he'd heard in the clubs in London many nights during what we Americans referred to as the British Invasion. Knowing how much he enjoyed many of the great rock bands from that era, I gave his music a chance, too, and we listened to many of his favorite songs together.

Of course, I'd had a different musical experience, having grown up in the states during the seventies and eighties. The music from that time was so much fun. Loud and crazy, with a lot of hair involved. I just loved it. Some of our tastes overlapped, and some didn't. He still teases me when he catches me listening to Seattle grunge (which I usually do in hiding.)

"Oh, how I worry about you," he says. I just laugh. We both make an effort to respect each other's taste in music. Our children have acquired a taste for both types of music, along with their own. So we can all have fun together in this area.

Look for ways to blend each other's interests while respecting the fact that each of you has different tastes. One way to determine whether a couple respects each other is by watching them communicate. Try to remember how you talked to each other as a new couple. I'm sure you were slow to anger and watched your words. Did you argue? Maybe not too often, especially in the beginning. Did you put your mate down or embarrass them? I bet you didn't. How you speak to your mate and how you support them can make or break your relationship.

Do you value their opinions? Remember when you asked their opinion on nearly everything? They were glad to give advice on nearly any subject, and were pleased that you were interested in what they had to say. Do you still ask them for advice, or have you decided your way is better? Try asking them more often for their point of view before you make a decision. They'll be so pleased you asked, even if you don't act on it exactly as they suggested. They'll still appreciate you valuing their opinion enough to consult them first. Always tell them how much their advice helped you make a decision.

PRIDE, GET BEHIND ME

How do you speak to your mate in front of others? Do you argue with their point of view? Pride can get us into so much trouble. We like to think we know what's best in every area, but the truth is this: Your mate has had plenty of life experiences, too. They may be just as smart as you or even smarter in many respects.

Do you question your mate in public or put them down? You may not realize this, but you're disrespecting them when you do this. Putting down your mate is a huge no-no. It's particularly hurtful when you do it in front of others. Pride can be a wicked tool with which to tear someone down. Some people do this to fill their need to be right. Some put others down in order to lift themselves up. Others are just in a bad mood and want someone else to take the brunt of their frustrations. Some crave attention, so they disregard others' opinions and feelings in order to keep the focus on them. Whatever the reason, it's wrong!

Always value what your mate has to say. It doesn't matter how minor the issue is. They'll appreciate the support, because sometimes that's the only place they'll get it. If they can't get positive support from their mate, they will surely look for it elsewhere.

I say, "Yes, dear" a lot. I try to show my hubby as much respect as I can, as often as I can. Sometimes, I'm tired and maybe not listening as attentively as I should be. I listen and respond in a somewhat encouraging way, as much as I can when I'm dozing off.

How do you speak to your friends and coworkers? Are you courteous, slow to anger and understanding with your friends? Do you let your friends speak a bit rudely to you at times and let it slide? Do you let your friends or coworkers correct you, maybe even boss you around, and just take it lightly? Do you let your friends take their frustrations of the day out on you and just brush it off?

How do you react when your mate has a bad day and yells at you? Do you bite their head off? If work or school is getting hard for your mate and they're tired and grouchy, do you let things go, or do you add to their aggravation and upset them even more? It's funny how we choose to treat those closest to us with little patience while letting others slide. We know our loved ones will put up with it, but they have limits, too.

I remember early in my marriage, I made such an effort to be nice to everyone. Then I'd come home at the end of a long week, and my hubby would get slammed with my grouchiness. He'd imitate me being kind to everyone else and then point out how I had no time or positive attention left for him. I always felt bad when that happened. I hadn't even realized I was doing it, and I'd correct it immediately. Put your mate's feelings at the top of your priority list when you're communicating.

LAUGH, LAUGH AND LAUGH SOME MORE

Do you still laugh together? This is one thing my hubby and I still do a lot. Often, we're retelling a story or remembering a funny line from a comedy on TV and reliving that laughter over and over. I continually get made fun of for telling the same stories over and over and laughing, time and time again. Yet people still ask me, "Can you tell that story to so-and-so? That one is so funny."

So here's one of my favorites I'd like to share. The coolest boy in the entire school actually saved my life in the seventh grade. One day after school, as we were getting on the bus to go home, I accidentally bumped into the girl in front of me. I was small and thin, weighing only about 75 pounds at that time. She was two years older than me, athletic and much bigger than I was. She turned around and hit me in the stomach so hard I dropped to the floor. I lay there, out of breath, wondering what had just happened. I felt like I was going to die.

The next day, I told the boy who lived across the street what had happened. I'll call him Pat. Pat was so popular at school and known as the coolest boy in our junior high. Everyone wanted to be his friend. He was nice to everyone, and so cute and funny.

I used to ask other kids, "Do you know Pat? He actually lives across the street from me and has been to my house for my birthday parties. I know him pretty well." Kids would say, "Wow, you're so lucky."

So I told Pat the whole story about what had happened to me on the bus. He said, "I'll take care of it." The next day after school at the bus stop, Pat walked up with two very large girls next to him, both standing close to six feet tall.

One was a big redhead, the other a very strong-looking Hispanic girl. I think they were a couple of years older than me. The rumor was that these girls had flunked ninth grade a few times, and that's why they were so much bigger than the rest of us. I think they were just really tall. What I really cared about was that they looked very intimidating.

Pat asked me which girl had hit me. I pointed her out, and Pat began to tell her, in front of a big crowd of kids, what these girls were going to do to her if she ever touched me again. I only remember some of what was said, something about her face being dragged across the cement.

Well, of course, the girl who'd hit me started to cry. The crowd of kids were yelling, "Fight, fight!" but Pat was kind and told her this was a warning. I was pleased, and she was thankful, and that was the end of that.

Many years have passed, and I've told that story to my kids and their friends so many times, about how I nearly died in the seventh grade. During a visit to my hometown many years later, we were staying with one of my girlfriends when the doorbell rang, and my then-teenage daughter answered it.

Parked in the driveway was a Harley motorcycle, and a man dressed in leather clothes was at the door. My daughter had never seen my dear friend, but as soon as she did, she said instinctively, "You must be Pat." I'd later learn that my girlfriend had called him. That day, my husband and my children finally got to meet my childhood hero. I love to tell that story. The memory always makes me laugh and smile.

Do you have fun stories that make others laugh? I bet you do. Are you too busy to share them? Take the time to laugh. It's so much fun. I don't care if I've told something over and over, my husband and I will laugh again about funny situations like we've just heard them for the first time.

Who says you can't laugh like you did when you were a kid? Who says you have to be so serious all the time? I can be serious when I need to be, but I prefer to be lighthearted and kind of silly. Time flies by. I don't want to waste it being negative and stressed and not enjoying each and every day.

You might be thinking that this all sounds pretty simple, but really involves a lot of changes and plenty of effort. You may also be telling yourself, what if I do these things and nothing changes? Don't worry. Most likely, it will. If you try to remain respectful, thoughtful, and fun-loving as much as possible, you should eventually get a positive response. It might take a while, but most likely, it will work.

YOU CANNOT CONTROL ANYONE ELSE, ONLY YOURSELF

I remember a woman I worked with years ago who didn't seem to care for me. I don't know why, but she never smiled at me. She often spoke rudely to me. I figured I had two choices. I could either ignore her, or I could be kind, light and funny with her. I chose the latter. For months, I did this with no change. It was very difficult, but I didn't stop trying to be her friend. Finally, one day I saw her laugh and crack a smile when I spoke to her.

From that day on, we got along beautifully. It took a lot of work and disappointment day after day, but in the end I learned that you can't control anyone else. You can only control yourself. Even the most difficult people may respond to being treated well, eventually. Obviously, my coworker was dealing with issues that had nothing to do with me, but I didn't give up. She stopped working with us not long after that, but I still think of her often.

How much more is your relationship with your mate worth to you? Are you willing to make the effort? If you're married, you promised to love and to cherish your spouse. So get busy loving and cherishing! In reality, it's really easy, much easier than not getting along, which actually takes much more of your energy and effort.

Let your lips shower your mate with kindness between your kisses. Lift them up with encouragement and cover them with sweet words. Then they will look forward to being with no one more than you.

Chapter 3
Appearance – Working with What You Have!

When you and your sweetie were dating, how much time did you spend on your appearance? Did you fix your hair for hours before a big party or night out at the clubs? I know I did. Was your makeup done just right, like you'd just had a makeover? Did you paint your nails, and then repaint them when the polish began to chip? Did your purse match your shoes? Did you select your jewelry carefully? Did you carefully plan your outfit each day, frantically searching for the perfect look?

It isn't just women that go out of their way to look their best for their date. Guys, you probably also made more of an effort to look nice for your mate back then. You tried harder to impress your love, and made sure that you were well-groomed. You pressed your shirts and wore well-fitting jeans. You made sure you had a stylish haircut and even added a touch of cologne so you would smell nice for her, too.

The effort we put into our appearance when we're dating is well worth it, because we know it pleases our love interest. When you're single, you want to look good, not just for yourself, but also for others who might be interested in you.

Remember the girl who always had a boyfriend in high school, the one who always looked so pretty all the time? Yes, we envied her. Was she really that much more attractive than the girl who came to school as she was?

Probably not. Very few women can walk out the door with nothing but a quick shower and look extremely attractive and put-together. If you're one of those people, you are truly lucky. I'm not one of them.

I'm sure the only real difference between that pretty girl and the one who came as she was came down to the effort each put in (or didn't put in) to enhance their appearance. The pretty girl had perfectly styled hair, where the other girl may have just combed hers. She arose early and applied her makeup carefully, but the other girl might not care for makeup at all. One color-coordinated her clothes and made sure they fit just right. The other probably selected her outfits based on what was comfortable and easy to wear.

Do your clothes give people the impression that you should be home cleaning a bathroom? If so, you've become way too relaxed in your choice of attire and your appearance. If what you're wearing is so comfortable you could sleep in it, you probably shouldn't be wearing it out of the house. This is especially important to address if you're in a relationship.

And it's not just the ladies that need to keep up appearances for their mates. Men, this goes for you, too! When you were younger, many of you went to the gym, got your hair styled regularly, and tried to coordinate your clothes. You worried about your appearance and cared about how you looked. As we get older and take on such busy schedules, these things take some effort, though not as much effort as you might think.

There are so many affordable ways to spruce up your appearance for next to nothing. Anyone can afford to spend a small amount of money to improve their look.

HAVE FUN WHILE ENHANCING YOUR APPEARANCE!

Enhancing your appearance doesn't have to be a lot of work. There's no reason it can't be fun, too. For example, one day, my daughter and I decided to get a pedicure for a special occasion. I wasn't very familiar with the whole mani/pedi experience, but I knew it was popular with the young girls, so we stopped by a nearby nail shop run by a group of nice Asian ladies.

As we sat side by side in the massage chairs soaking our feet, we listened to the ladies chatting away in their own language as a young girl helped me and an older woman attended to my daughter.

Halfway through the process, I heard the young girl say something to the older woman. The woman quickly looked over at my legs and then quickly looked back with her head down.

I asked, "What did you just say?"

The girl responded, "You *taw.*" (*You're tall.*)

"That's not what you said!" I answered, before turning to my daughter and saying, "This is just like that Seinfeld episode where the Korean ladies in the nail shop make fun of Elaine."

We both started laughing hysterically.

Confused, the women stopped, looked at us and asked, *"Ticko?"*

Like the reason we were laughing was that she was tickling me.

I answered, "Yeah, *ticko.*"

We had a lot of fun that day and spent a little time on our appearance as well. Take an extra moment or two to try a new look or something new. Have fun with it.

PHASES – HOW OUR LOOK CHANGES

We all change as we get older and our lives change. The key is to enjoy each phase and make the best of it. I remember when my kids were growing up, I went through the dreaded "Mom" stage. Back then, I wore baggy summer jumpsuits or sleeveless long dresses that fell way below the knee. One day, when my oldest son was in his early teens, I arrived to pick him up from a pizza party. His eyes nearly jumped out of his head when he saw me. I was wearing my favorite bright red, polka-dot sleeveless jumpsuit and pointy, flat white shoes. My son hated that outfit.

On the walk to the car, he could hardly breathe. He started yelling from the moment we drove off and didn't let up for the next 20 minutes. How could I have let his classmates see me in that outfit? Didn't I know how embarrassing that would be for him? He said he was going to have to change schools now, because obviously, he could never face his friends again. One of my girlfriends jokes to this day that she and I should wear matching red-polka dot ensembles to my son's wedding someday. I still have that outfit in my closet, just in case.

We all go through phases as styles and trends change. How much time do you spend planning your daily outfits? When I was growing up, I remember my mother always applied brightly colored lipstick before she went out. I have continued that tradition. I don't think I've ever been seen out in public without lipstick.

My mother also wouldn't go out without big, dangly earrings. She's nearly 80 years old now and still has a huge collection of flashy earrings. As I've been writing this chapter, I've made a conscious effort to observe other women, and I've been pleased to see that many put a lot of effort into their appearance. Yet we can all make improvements and maybe try something new every once in a while. After all, who doesn't look good after a makeover? No one.

It only takes a moment to change your appearance. Put on something that makes you look slimmer, curvier or taller, and your entire look, and possibly your outlook, will change immediately.

Has your appearance changed much since your relationship began? I'm not talking about your physical appearance. We all change with time. Nature catches up with all of us. I'm talking about your style.

A woman I know in her early 90's often sports freshly-painted black nail polish. That always catches my eye immediately. She tells me her granddaughter does her nails.

One day I told her, "I like the black nails look on you."

"It's a good look for the fall," she answered.

"You go, honey," I said.

This lady is in her nineties and still showcasing her own unique style. I've always had the impression she was a bit feisty when she was young. Imagine how great it would be to be that age and still willing to try different things to enhance your look.

Has anyone ever mistaken you for your child's grandparent? I've told my husband that looking good at our age and as we get older is going to take a lot of work, but I'm willing to put in the effort. Think about that the next time you consider wearing nice, comfortable loafers instead of more stylish shoes. You're not wearing those casual, elastic-waist slacks, are you? It's always nice to be comfortable, but come on, ladies!

Let's put some effort into our appearance. No more looking like someone no one ever quite remembers! Spend a day making a short list of ways you can improve your appearance, and then do it! You'll be glad you did. You'll feel better, and your mate will be thrilled.

PLEASING YOUR MATE WITH YOUR LOOK

The next question you should ask yourself is what does your mate like you to wear? Maybe he likes you in a dress, a nice skirt, or even a youthful bathing suit. You may not feel like dressing that way anymore, but you should really do it, anyway.

Take out that dress your honey loves. Buy that skirt that flatters your shape so nicely. There are so many bathing suit styles available for women of all shapes and sizes. You can even mix and match tops and bottoms to hide imperfections or make you look slimmer. The point is to do it!

If you're wearing a tee shirt every day, stop now. Some people look really good in them, but most of us don't fall into that category. Nice jeans are my favorite, since they're so easy to dress up with some fun accessories. A bright necklace with matching earrings, a bracelet and some fun heels go a long way.

Do you dress up a little when you go out, even if you're just running to the grocery store or the mall? Why not? Try it. If you get in the habit of dressing up a bit to go anywhere, your honey will notice and greatly appreciate it, too. You can buy a variety of accessories for next to nothing. I often get these items at the flea market. I have a large selection that didn't cost me much at all.

I've heard men ask their mates why they don't wear that special dress they like so much, or put on their favorite outfit. Listen to your mate's needs and follow through. They need to know that you care about your appearance, because it tells them you care about them and their needs, too.

And men, if your mate takes a long time to get ready, be patient with her. One day in the future, you'll be glad she spends time on her appearance for you. And make sure you put in the same level of effort with your own appearance. Are you wearing the same clothes you wore ten years ago? We feel the same way you do. We like a man who's nicely put together.

There's nothing wrong with holding onto a few fashions from the past. Pick your favorites and combine them with some modern styles. Some clothes are classic and will always be in style. I like to mix in my favorite styles from the eighties – a little velvet, a little tie-dye, and plenty of fun patterns combined with today's looks. When people say I'm stuck in the past, I smile and take it as a compliment. So dress up, but be yourself, too.

Remember this: your appearance is what made your mate first notice you. Keep this in mind as you look for ways to enhance your look and have fun doing it!

Chapter 4
Beneficial Friendships and Dealing with the Past

Do you have relationships with others that benefit you and your mate? We all enjoy the company of others. If you have friends or family you gather with regularly, you know what a treat those times are. You always have the most fun when you're in great company. I know I do.

What's also important to remember is that along with these fun times comes responsibility. Choose your friends carefully.

Don't let anyone enter your social circle if they might harm your relationship.

Do you have friends who put your sweetheart down? Limit your time with those types of people if at all possible. Set them straight and let them know you won't tolerate any disrespect toward your mate. Then ask them to keep their opinions to themselves. Your commitment to your mate is more important than any one friend.

FIND A BALANCE BETWEEN YOUR MATE, FRIENDS AND ACTIVITIES

Having a lot of friends is great, as long as it doesn't cause problems in your relationship. Of course, if you take your friendships to the extreme and spend too much time away from your mate, that can cause significant problems in your relationship. Do you spend more time with your friends than you do with your mate?

Are you overextending yourself? Do you volunteer to help out at school and spend all your time handling after-school activities? Are you the soccer mom, the karate mom, and the dance class mom? Do you spend so much time with everyone else that you have little energy and time left for your mate?

Don't spread yourself too thin by trying to do everything. Let your friends organize the next cookout. Host your next birthday party somewhere where they do most of the work for you. Is it time for a girls' night out? Keep it reasonable, not until all hours of the night. It's just as much fun to get together for a few hours.

EVERYONE KNOWS YOUR BUSINESS

Do you share all of your intimate problems with your girlfriends? Those should really stay between you and your mate. If you share too much with your friends and family, they'll lose their objectivity where your mate is concerned. Pour your heart out to them in the midst of an argument and they'll want to take your side. Unfortunately, they may still have hard feelings toward your mate long after the argument has subsided, which will create even more problems than your disagreement with your mate did.

If you need to vent, share with an unbiased person who's not close to the situation, preferably someone who doesn't know your mate. Choose someone who won't gossip about your personal life, and don't request advice from someone who has a lot of their own problems. Misery loves company, and sometimes, miserable people want to bring someone down with them. Just remember that there are boundaries for every situation. I love having lots of friends and staying busy, but my hubby always comes first.

Do you have a friend who's a little too friendly toward your mate? Tell them directly that's unacceptable and inappropriate. Don't put yourselves in situations that could put your relationship at risk.

Do you work with a lot of members of the opposite sex? Keep those relationships at a proper distance. If you don't want to put your relationship at risk, don't start a relationship that could go in that direction. Limit your conversations to basic topics when in these situations.

If you don't give someone extra attention, they'll seek it elsewhere! If possible, don't ever be alone with someone you find engaging or attractive. I'm usually friendly to everyone. I can talk with people I've just met like I've known them for twenty years. Sometimes, people interpret that kind of friendliness to mean something else. If a man takes my chattiness the wrong way, I quickly bring up my husband. That usually ends that problem immediately.

NO FLIRTING ALLOWED!

Do you have a wandering eye? Like to flirt a bit when you're out and about? If you do, you need to stop! I always tell my husband that I don't really know which type of woman he favors, because I've never seen him look at another woman, not even when we were dating. He's that thoughtful of my feelings. I tell him the only women I know that he likes are Cher and Chrissie Hynde from The Pretenders. He just smiles and says *I'm* his type. Good answer!

If flirting is really a problem for you, you need to get a hold of yourself. As we mature, we can control our actions. You have a choice not to do this and risk upsetting your mate. If you're overly friendly with someone, or dress too suggestively when you go out, you're sending the wrong message and potentially putting your relationship at risk. This is straight-out asking for trouble. It also shows no respect for your mate.

No flirting allowed, period.

Are you still in touch with people from your past? This is fine, as long as you keep those friendships at a safe distance, preferably a lot of distance. I still stay in contact with some of my friends from my youth. I've known some of them since kindergarten. I've always told my husband about male friends I've heard from, and when I see them (which is not very often,) it's always in a group setting.

Fortunately, he's very friendly and treats the friends I grew up with like they were his childhood friends as well. If your mate isn't comfortable with you staying friendly with people from your past, it's best to respect their feelings and limit those relationships.

SOCIAL MEDIA

Do you spend a lot of time on the Internet, getting sucked into social networks? I know I have. It's a lot of fun chatting with your high school and college friends and getting caught up. Be careful, though, if it starts to cut into your time with your mate. You need to limit yourself. Make sure your conversations are appropriate, If you're chatting with people online, be courteous of others' feelings, both your mate's and your friends' spouses.

Maintain boundaries in your conversations. If you have been exchanging adult jokes, be careful. If you're married or your friends are, you could be disrespecting your spouse and theirs. Don't send the wrong message. Think before you chat. We all need to be careful of our words. Do you really think your mate is okay with you having adult chitchat with someone else? Don't take any chances with your relationship.

VALUE THE PAST

Does it upset you when your mate talks about someone from his past? This can be especially awkward if you're in a situation where they have to stay in touch with each other.

My husband and I have always had an unspoken rule. No talking badly about someone from our past. We never had to tell each other this. We just did it.

There are two ways to look at your mate's past. You can drive yourself crazy comparing yourself to his past loves. You can wonder about all of the fun they had together and ask yourself why they're with you now instead of them. But there's no point to thinking this way. Your mate didn't even know you existed before he met you. He was free to meet and enjoy anyone who crossed his path.

I prefer the other way of looking at your mate's past. Value each person from their past and acknowledge the influence they must have had on them. They helped mold them into the person they've become, the one you're now enjoying! Our past makes up who we are. I care for each woman my husband dated before me, because I realize they made him happy at that point in his life and made his life richer before I came into it.

I pray for the ones I know of and think of them as part of my life, too. Whoever is or was important to my husband is important to me now, also. It took some time for me to get to this point, but it is so freeing. Give thanks for the people from your past.

Do you speak poorly about someone from your mate's past? If so, stop now. It doesn't benefit anyone, and in the end, it only makes you feel bad. Putting someone else down just to lift yourself up indicates a deeper issue, one that's more about you than it is about them. A wicked tongue cuts only inward. There's no good reason to put others down if your mate once cared for them. This takes some maturity to accomplish, but it can be done.

If you have children from a previous relationship, they don't need to hear bad things about their other parent, especially now that they may not be around all of the time. This is even more important if someone else has taken their place. Your children didn't ask for this situation. So put their needs before your own. Keep your mouth shut and keep the peace for your kid's sake and the sake of the family.

Value your children's father or mother and show respect for them, even if you're no longer together. Your kids are watching your actions, and will learn more from what you do than what you say. People are watching you every day, whether you realize it or not. Be a good example from whom others might learn.

WHO DOESN'T WANT BETTER?

Have the two of you been together for a while? As time goes by, you may believe you have to settle for a relationship that began full of excitement and joy, but is now just "okay." But why settle for that when you can have better?

A friend once told me that of all of her married friends, only two were truly happily married. When I asked who they were, she said, "You're one." When I asked who the second one was, I expected her to name one of her other girlfriends. Instead, she named my husband. I was floored. I know a lot of people who are content in their marriage, but you can always make improvements in any relationship. Who doesn't want better? You can't change anyone else, but you can certainly change yourself.

FUN WITH CLOSE FRIENDS AND FAMILY

Do you have good friends you like to visit with? Having good friends and family to enjoy free time with is one of the great treats of this life! No one knows you better than a childhood friend or family member. They've watched you do the stupidest things, things you can now laugh about. My family knows I love to laugh over old stories. I also love to gather with the girlfriends from my youth. For weeks, we'll plan our get-togethers, and I so look forward to seeing them. We laugh about all the crazy things we did back in high school and college.

Here's one funny story they love to tease me about:

Once, we were invited to a large party being held by a group of young high school guys. They were students at an exclusive, elite all-boys prep school in town, and the party was held at a large home on the other side of town. My girlfriends were so excited to be invited to this party, and had looked forward to it for weeks. They arrived early and were having a great time meeting all these nice, eligible young boys.

I decided to show up later with my date and his brother, who I'd only just met a few hours before. My date had long, blond hair and was wearing jeans, a concert tee shirt and brown suede fringed knee boots that I thought were so cool.

I hadn't really noticed that my new friends may have seemed out of place – a couple of rock n' rollers socializing at a party with these straight-laced boys. Well, not long after we arrived, we were asked to leave. I guess we didn't fit in at the party. My girlfriends were asked to leave as well, and still yell at me to this day about it. That party was over thirty years ago, but they still talk about it. We laugh every time, and I always say, "I had a blast! I'd do it again!"

The funniest thing about that story is that I have a shoebox full of things from my youth, and I recently found a small 2-inch scrap of paper with that young man's name and address on it. He'd been visiting on vacation when I met him at the mall where I worked. I guess I was supposed to write him after that night. Sorry, Dave from Massachusetts! I may not have written, but you have not been forgotten.

I'm lucky I have mostly good memories from my dating years and all the craziness that goes along with it. All the boys I knew were great fun. I remember each one of them and treasure those times.

Do you have friends or family you gather with just to laugh and have a good time? Make the time to do this. It's so much fun to go back in time and relive the crazy things you did in the past or even something funny that happened last week.

THE OPPORTUNITY IS NOW!

I have a large Hispanic family. We say we're like a big Greek family, because when we get together, we get so loud you can't hear anything else. My husband always laughs and says, "Why are they fighting?" I always explain that they're not fighting. That's just the way they talk. He's always trying to fit in, speaking Spanish in his still-strong British accent.

When we talk about things from the past, the stories get a little more exaggerated each time they're told, which, of course, makes them even funnier. Someone usually puts on some music, and before you know it, everyone's dancing in the living room. It's always a riot when my mother, uncles and aunts, all of who are approaching or in their seventies, show us how to really dance. Of course, the younger ones usually watch and wonder what the heck they're doing.

If you don't have get-togethers like these very often, you're missing out. Make the effort to gather with family and friends more often. Otherwise, you'll blink and this time will be gone. Don't waste it! The opportunity is now!

I'm also fortunate enough to work with a wonderful group of people whose company I really enjoy. We have great fun together. Many of us get along well and have become great friends. We love to have outings together during the summer on our days off. Workplace friendships should enrich your time at work and make it more enjoyable.

SUPPORT AT ANY TIME, FOR ANYTHING

Do you have a church family? If you don't, let me tell you how much this can bless your life. My church family brings food when someone's sick. They're there to chat whenever I need them. They're happy to help any of our friends, even if they don't know them. My pastor's father has been our personal handyman for many years, never charging us a dime. Whenever he completes a project, he says, "Just give a little something to the church."

Our church family has given time, support and money whenever they saw a need, day or night. I can call almost anyone from my church family, at any time, for anything and find someone who's willing to help.

Do you have this kind of support from God's people? If you don't, it's never too late to join a good church. The blessings you receive as part of a welcoming, supportive church family are only one part of it. When you help others, that's when the true blessings begin.

If your mate is your only source of emotional support, the one who takes on all of your burdens, you're putting way too much on his or her shoulders. Keep your support group large. You can never have too many close friends. My daughter has asked many times,

"Who's your best friend?" My answer is always the same. I have about twenty best friends.

My large family is great. We're always there for each other. My mother, brother, sister, aunts, uncles and cousins will offer to help with anything or give support when needed. My children, nieces, nephews and young cousins are learning from the adults how family will always be there for you. They're starting to realize how important their family is. I'm happy to see them start to build on these relationships. Never neglect your family and friends. One day, they may become the only place you can turn to.

Chapter 5
Fighting Constructively

Do you and your mate fight often? If you both have strong personalities, the fighting probably began after you'd been dating for a little while. In the beginning, you probably let things slide. After a while, you got comfortable, and probably nothing got past you then. I didn't learn how to fight constructively until I was well into my marriage.

When we were newly married, my husband and I argued often. It was always loud, and we were both strong-willed and disrespectful of each other. When we began having children, we quickly realized our fighting was not going to have a good effect on them. Slowly, we learned not to argue in front of them. Then we learned not to curse at each other and to discuss issues more calmly. This process evolved slowly over the course of several years.

Fighting can destroy a relationship and influence your children in an extremely negative way. If you're fighting a lot, you can choose to do it in a calmer manner. My husband calls this "constructive negotiating."

TONE IT DOWN!

Cursing and insulting each other gets you nowhere fast, because your mate will stop listening to what you're saying once it starts. It doesn't matter whether you're fighting over money, the kids, housework or anything else. How you say things is the key. You can't change your mate's way of fighting, but you can change yourself and the way you communicate.

Only you can choose to disagree in a calmer manner that will eventually help your mate respond differently. If one of you is screaming and the other remains calm, eventually the one who's losing control will do it less. It takes two to have an argument, and it's no fun for the one screaming. If you don't react, and they see they're not getting a reaction out of you, they'll eventually begin to see how unreasonably they're acting.

Some people will never change, no matter what you do, but most people will respond to being treated respectfully, since that's their real need, whether they realize it or not. They need to be heard and treated with respect.

If they start yelling, immediately ask them to discuss things in a quiet manner if they want the conversation to continue. If this happens in front of your children, go into another room where they can't hear what's being said. Children that hear a disagreement between their parents will often use this information to play one parent against the other. Those little cuties are good at this! Don't give them this opportunity to cause more problems between the two of you.

APOLOGIZE! YES, YOU CAN!

Implement the 5-15 minute rule. If you start to get aggravated with each other, and realize you're about to argue, take five minutes to collect your thoughts and then apologize. It doesn't matter whether the issue is your fault or theirs. Apologize that you were rude or short with your mate. If you're strong-willed, do it within fifteen to twenty minutes. Apologize for being disrespectful or yelling.

Since my husband and I learned to do this, we haven't had a real fight in years. Our children say they've never seen us really have a fight. Luckily, they were too little to remember the arguments we had when they were young. They're young adults now, and have seen us use the 5-15 minute rule. If I'm a little rude or annoyed because I'm feeling tired or grumpy, I quietly apologize within five minutes. It doesn't matter who is in the wrong. When I'm being really stubborn, I tell myself I must stop and apologize within fifteen minutes, or at the latest, thirty minutes. And we never scream at each other in front of others – ever.

Several of my longtime friends have said they've never heard me say anything negative or disrespectful about my husband. It's a choice to do this.

YOU DON'T KNOW WHAT YOU HAVEN'T TRIED

You might be thinking, "But my mate will never change. He's always been hot-tempered and will always be this way." That may be true in some cases, but you simply don't know unless you try. For a lot of people, positive communication and behavior is contagious. How many times have you seen someone being funny and making someone else laugh? Eventually, you can make even the grouchiest people in the room crack a smile if you keep the laughter going. Always remember that your behavior, mood and tone affect other people, good or bad.

If you start meeting your mate's needs, especially something that's as important to them as being respectful and agreeable, they'll respond differently in a positive way. It may be a slow process, but they'll start to feel differently each time you're kind, and they'll soften more and more. As time goes on, encouragement and better communication will feed a need in anyone, eventually affecting them in a positive way. The more you do this, the more they will respond.

GROWNUP COMMUNICATION

It takes some maturity to begin making these types of changes in your relationship. If you're young, start being respectful to your mate now and use these constructive negotiating tools. You'll be well ahead of the game if you begin a long-term relationship with beneficial ways to negotiate and remain kind to one another instead of fighting. You'll get nowhere but upset without these techniques.

If you're older, but not really mature enough to make these kinds of changes, grow up and get busy! Yes, swallow your pride, because that's the real issue that's keeping you from changing.

Pride is the root of nearly all problems. Swallow, stomp, and get rid of your prideful ways. They accomplish nothing and damage everything that's good in our lives. It's funny how people believe that the louder they get, the more they will accomplish, when in reality, the louder you get, the less people hear what you're saying. Eventually, they just totally tune you out altogether. You don't want your mate to tune you out.

IF THAT'S YOUR WORST PROBLEM, YOU'RE DOING PRETTY GOOD

My next question is, "What are you fighting about?" I'm sure you've heard the saying, "Don't sweat the small stuff, because it's all small stuff." There's enormous truth to that saying. Have you ever gotten in a fight with your mate and then wondered afterward, "What was *that* all about?"

We waste so much energy worrying about such trivial things. My favorite saying is, "If that's your worst problem, you're doing pretty good." My middle son used to get so upset when I said that to him. He'd just stare at me when I said it. He's an analytical young man, and always thoroughly thinks every little thing through to the last detail. So that saying just didn't fly for him.

Of course, I wasn't trying to minimize his feelings or concerns. I was just trying to get him to look at things from a lighter perspective.

I've jokingly told my husband that I want that saying engraved on my tombstone so people can walk by my grave, alive and well, and read, "If that's your worst problem, you're doing pretty good." Does anyone else find that extremely humorous?

I try to take most things lightly. I may occasionally get annoyed just like anyone else, but I try to stay encouraging most of the time and not let little things bother me too much. Once, when one of my childhood girlfriends traveled from Wisconsin to Florida to visit me, she left a pair of her shoes by my front door when she left. Now, I have a row of shoes behind my front door at all times. I only move them when I vacuum, and then I move them back when I'm done. Well, she returned to visit the following year, and found her shoes in the same spot exactly as she'd left them, just a bit dustier.

When she saw them, she said, "El! I thought I'd lost those shoes. I can't believe they're still sitting there where I left them. Didn't you notice them?" We started laughing hysterically, and she just shook her head, repeating my childhood nickname. "El, El, El," the same way she always does when I do something that amuses her. I'd probably thought those were my daughter's shoes lying there, and assumed she didn't wear them often. But even when I learned of my mistake, I thought it was hysterical. I wasn't upset or embarrassed in the least.

Do you get upset with yourself or your mate over little things that aren't really worth fussing over, or do you laugh things off?

My husband *loves* to tell me how to drive.

"Turn this way."

"Get in the other lane."

"You'll need to change lanes soon. Don't wait too long."

I've learned not to say much in response. I drive the way he wants me to. Sometimes, I jokingly make fun of him and remind him that I've been driving since I was sixteen and know what I'm doing. But most of the time, I just follow his instructions. He's pleased, and we maintain a pleasant environment in the car. It's easy.

So many fights start over things that aren't worth mentioning. Do you really need to make your mate feel bad when things don't turn out just right? No, you don't. Maybe it's something they really worked hard on, and your reaction could really hurt them. Start to let some of those things go, and you'll see your relationship grow much more peaceful.

Do you call your mate names or curse at them when you fight? This is a big no-no. Don't use any derogatory names or long, drawn-out expletives. Negotiate fairly. Name calling is nasty and harsh. You'll never win an argument that way. You don't want your mate to wonder,

"What am I doing with this person?" If that's how you argue, you're losing control. Take a deep breath and tone it down, for everyone's sake.

Do you bring up disagreements from the past? Are you one of those people that continue to relive unpleasant events from last year's Christmas party or some vacation you took five years ago? If so, remember that no one can change something they did in the past, no matter how much they might want to.

It doesn't matter if it happened last month or ten years ago. Bringing up a mistake or wrongdoing that happened long ago is pointless. If, by some chance, you can bring up something positive about it, then it might be acceptable. If not, it's best to leave these issues in the past.

During an argument, if you hear yourself saying, "I remember when you did this," stop right then and refocus on what's happening right now. Keep all issues current. If your disagreements have escalated to the point of being physical, seek help outside the home. Reach out to an organization that specializes in helping victims of physical abuse.

"I CAN'T" REALLY MEANS "I WON'T"

This is one of the most important parts of getting along with your mate. If you can do this, the benefits will trickle down to every aspect of your relationship in such a positive way. Do you ever hear yourself saying this?

"I *can't* stop yelling."

"He makes me so mad, I *can't* stay calm. He's such an idiot."

And the ever-popular, ""I *can't* change who I am."

What you're really saying here is that you *won't* stop yelling. You *won't* try to stay calm. You *refuse* to change.

In reality, what you're refusing to do is so simple. What's holding you back? Once again, it's your pride and stubbornness. Stop saying, "I *can't*" when what you really mean is you *won't*.

Make an effort to put aside your pride and start making changes in the way you get along and resolve differences with your mate. Try some constructive negotiating so you can gain all of the wonderful benefits of a healthy, happy relationship.

Chapter 6
Managing Finances

How do you and your mate handle financial issues? Are you living above your means? That's a pretty common problem. We all want a beautiful house, a nice car and stylish clothes, and it can be difficult to control your spending when there are so many temptations out there. It's so easy to convince ourselves we've just got to have that large flat-screen TV, that shiny new sports car, or the newest techie gadget. Society tells us that we need all of these things and simply can't live without them.

We have a large, old-fashioned Magnavox TV in our living room. It probably weighs a hundred pounds! The screen is huge, and the picture is great. When my cousin came to visit recently, her young son saw it and asked, "Why do you have a chalkboard in your living room?"

My children have asked me over and over again to get rid of that old dinosaur and buy a large flat-screen TV, but I always say, "Why would I get a new one when the TV I have works fine?" The picture is plenty big enough, and the television works great. I tell them that when it breaks, that's when I'll move onto a flat screen. That may be next week, or if I'm lucky, five years from now. They just shake their heads.

YO-YO FINANCIAL LIFESTYLES

Do you like to spend money? Who doesn't like to go out and buy something they really want? You know that saying, "Don't go grocery shopping when you're hungry?" Well, the same goes for going into stores filled with items you know you can't afford.

Why shop at Macy's when your paycheck says, "Go to Wal-Mart?" If you have the willpower to window-shop without temptation, then it's not a problem. But why walk so close to that fine jewelry counter? It's not your birthday. The next time the mood strikes, pick up some inexpensive costume jewelry instead.

Buying new shoes again? Why? Do you have 30 pairs already? How many do you need to maintain a stylish wardrobe? I have the opposite problem. I probably only have about four or five pairs of shoes. I try to make them work with every outfit I have, wearing them until they start to fall apart, and then wearing them just a few weeks longer. That's one of the issues *I* need to work on!

Your mate could be tempted to spend as well. Men often long for shiny motorcycles or cars, or maybe even a brand-new boat if you live near the water, like we do. Often, men will put a boat up for sale after only using it a few times because the gas is so expensive. The key is for both of you to curb your spending on luxury items and nonessentials. That way, you'll have money left over for what you really need.

Do you often buy things you could really do without and then panic when you can barely pay your bills? That's what happens when you choose to live a yo-yo financial lifestyle. I'm far from perfect in my spending habits, but I'm downright excited that my husband and I haven't used our credit cards in a couple of years. We still have a balance on them, but I'm confident we'll have them paid off someday.

One way I've chosen to save money each month is by not carrying a cell phone. I know that in this day and age, that might be hard to believe! My husband keeps an inexpensive model just for emergencies. We buy prepaid minutes for it instead of keeping a contract. The money we save helps pay for our weekly movie dates and even a good concert here and there. This tiny sacrifice helps pay for those fun evenings out for the two of us.

I really enjoy my times out and about with no phone. It's my time to myself, when I can listen to some good music with no interruptions. Most people feel the need to carry a cell phone, and that's fine. You can find many other ways to save money each month if you sit and think about it.

Once, I was heading to the beach for two days for a class reunion with some of my girlfriends from high school. We took two cars, and for some reason I can't remember, I ended up driving in front, and they were following behind in another car. Whenever I drive for an extended period of time and some of my favorite music comes on (usually Journey or

Frampton,) I apparently get so relaxed that my driving slows down – drastically.

When we finally arrived at our beachfront hotel, my friend got out of her car and said, "Do you know how slow you were driving? I got flipped off so many times!"

Well, I'd never noticed how slow I was going. I explained, "Some good eighties music came on, and you know..."

Of course, she hadn't been able to call to tell me how slow I was driving during the hour-plus drive, since I don't have a cell phone. She laughed and then said, "What's that?"

I didn't know what she was talking about. "What?"

She pointed. "Your luggage," she said, pointing to the two Wal-Mart bags I'd thrown in the car in lieu of luggage.

"You know, we're checking into an upscale hotel," she smiled.

"It's not like we're going on a cruise. We're here for two days," I explained.

We all started laughing, and I happily walked into the hotel with a big smile on my face, Wal-Mart bags and all. The running joke all weekend was whether everyone had seen my matching luggage.

It's easy to save money if you simply give up the things you don't really need. Do you drive a car that costs you a fortune each month? You can drive a used car that still looks really nice and saves you a lot of money. Shopping at the best stores and buying all the best brands? There's nothing wrong with that if you can afford it. But if you can't, buying off-brands and shopping at discount stores are great alternatives.

Do you ever use your credit cards to buy things you can't really afford? Try to pay cash as much as possible. I've been doing it, and it feels great.

I've always loved shopping at the neighborhood discount grocery store. For many years, I drove into some not-so-popular neighborhoods just so I could get my groceries at a discount. I love a bargain, and don't care where I have to go to get it. Of course, my kids didn't want to be seen in these stores, so I always went alone. I can't imagine how much money I saved over the years doing that. Luckily, I have one of those stores close by now, so I can go almost daily.

We often choose to put ourselves in drastic financial situations and then can't figure out how we got there. We look for someone else to blame. Most of the time, you need to look at yourself and admit that you did the damage all on your own. Then start over and make some changes in the way you spend your money.

Do you hold onto your money tightly for yourself? I've found that if you help someone in need when the opportunity arises, it comes back to bless you even more.

IT'S ALL ABOUT HOW MUCH MONEY IS GOING OUT, NOT COMING IN

I often see people making high incomes who have about the same amount of extra money as those with much lower incomes. They're just as stressed out as the others, and for the same reason: they have no extra money.

I've often wondered how can that be? I've come to the conclusion that you don't have to make a lot of money to live well. It's all about how much money is going out, rather than what's coming in.

If you can learn this lesson, the benefits are huge. If you can keep your mortgage amount low, refinance when you can. Keep your car payment to a minimum, trade your car in or pay cash for a nice used car. Buy your clothes on sale or clearance, or my favorite, at the thrift store. We have a great thrift store for the young people here in town. Most young people buy their clothes at the best stores and then turn them in for extra money at this trendy store. The clothes haven't usually been worn much. I love to shop there. The average price for a new blouse is only about three to six dollars – a super deal!

When planning a vacation, do you really need to stay at the most expensive hotel, or is a smaller, less expensive motel what you really need? If you like to go out to dinner often, try going out to lunch instead. It's often cheaper and usually just as nice.

Most of us have to work. When my kids got older and began to complain about going to work, I would say, "That's why they call it going to work, not going to fun."

Stop blaming everyone else if you're in a tight financial situation. Most likely, no one else is to blame for it, unless you lost your job. Remember that you're the one who wanted that expensive house with the high mortgage payment. Who made you buy that fancy car that costs you a bundle each month? Who made you buy that boat, those designer clothes, the expensive watches and jewelry?

Of course, no one made you buy anything. You did this to yourself. Stop blaming others for your financial mess. Just admit it. Take a deep breath, make some changes and start living in a more relaxed way. It's so worth it! Remember it's not really about the amount of money that's coming in, as long as you're working. It's the amount of money going out that's the key.

I had the opportunity a few years ago to come into what I call "big money." One day, as I was leaving the mall with my daughter and her best girlfriend, I looked outside and saw that the sky was dark and threatening. Clearly, it was about to rain.

I yelled to the girls behind me to run for the elevator to the parking garage so we could beat the rain. I reached the elevator first. Suddenly, my legs flew out from underneath me and I fell flat on my back onto the elevator floor. The girls were several feet behind me, and running at an angle, so they could only see my head. They both panicked, thinking I had fallen down the elevator shaft.

An older man had been laying down tile in the elevator and just applied a sticky adhesive to the floor, which I'd slipped on. He ran over to me.

"Didn't you see the sign?" he said.

"What sign?" I asked.

He pointed to the wall so I could see the sign inside the elevator. Of course, the sign hadn't been visible from the angle where I'd started running from the mall. I got up, covered in sticky, white glue from head to toe. It was even on my purse.

The gentleman said, "I'm going to have to make a report. You'll have to come with me to the mall office."

I said, "I'm not walking through the mall like this. You'll have to ask your boss to come here."

So he left to get the mall manager. As we waited, it started raining, and we were all getting soaked. When the manager arrived, he was very concerned, holding an umbrella over his very expensive suit.

"Are you alright?" he asked.

I said, "I'm fine, but my clothes are ruined."

"I'm so sorry about that. Is there anything I can get for you?" he asked.

"A mall gift certificate would be nice," I said.

He immediately retrieved a $50 gift card, wrote his report, took some pictures and told me that the corporate office would be calling me in a few days to make sure I was still okay.

"Is there anything else I can do?" he asked before leaving.

"Yes. I want your umbrella," I answered.

Now, we were already soaked, but he handed me his umbrella as he stood there in the rain wearing that nice suit. We giggled as we walked up the stairs to my car. By this time, the gooey glue had soaked through my clothes, so I told the girls I was going to have to take my clothes off and put plastic on the seat of the car so it wouldn't be ruined from the glue.

The girls panicked. "What if someone from school sees you taking off your clothes?"

I explained that I was wearing a tank top under my shirt and would just undress down to my tank top and underwear.

By this time, we were laughing so hard that we could barely catch our breath. When we got home, I walked in the door, barefoot, dressed only in my underwear and tank top with a plastic bag stuck to my behind!

My husband and son, sitting on the couch, asked, "What happened to you?" as they tried not to laugh.

The next day, I was sore and limping a bit at the nursing home where I work. When my coworkers asked what had happened, I told them the whole story. They laughed and joked that I should have stayed down on the elevator floor and called Carter & Carter, one of our local law firms.

According to them, I hadn't fallen at just any mall. I'd taken a spill at the "good" mall. They could hardly stop laughing and carrying on about how I wouldn't have to go to work anymore, and that the mall's name would have to be changed to Marielle's Mall.

Well, I suppose I could have made a lot of money that day, but the bottom line was that I wasn't really hurt. The corporate office did call me in a few days, just as the manager had promised. I was honest and told them I wasn't hurt. They offered to pay for my clothes and anything that had been damaged.

When they asked me what the items were worth, I immediately thought that I'd probably gotten some of those things at the thrift store, so I said, "I don't know. What's the average price for a shirt, skirt, shoes, purse and underwear?" We both decided $150 was a fair amount, and they sent me a check. I was thrilled.

I suppose I could have made a lot of money that day, at someone else's expense. Do you ever do things to get ahead that cost someone else or hurt them in any way? It's not worth it. I have a clear conscience and a funny story I love to tell and laugh about. That's worth more to me than any amount of money I could have gotten by being less than truthful.

One way or another, it will always come back to bite you when you do wrong. So earn your money by working hard. Don't cheat anyone or hurt anyone to get ahead. You can really do it yourself.

We have so much to be thankful for. If you have a roof over your head, clothes on your back, and food to eat, you're really not poor. You may be struggling, but you're not poor.

And if by chance you do come into some "big money," think before you react. Resist the temptation to spend it right away. Taking a moment to think about the best way to use the money will help you make better decisions.

Instead of buying a fancy new car that will lose value the moment you drive it off the lot, consider investing the money instead. Put it toward something that will grow in value if you can. A small rental property that puts an extra $300 into your bank account each month could add up to $90,000 over 25 years. The value of the property itself may go up as well. You'll feel a lot better knowing that you used the money wisely.

Just keep in mind that having more money is not the secret to having a successful relationship. Continue to work hard, spend within your means, and enjoy your free time in inexpensive ways. Your life will be richer for it, and your relationship with your mate will be much stronger and less stressful.

Chapter 7
Roles and Responsibilities

Does your household run smoothly, or do you have two people both trying to be in charge of the same household, with one trying to control the other and vice versa? You cannot have two people at the head of the family. Just as we have one president and one vice president, managers and assistant managers, head coaches and assistant coaches, you need the same hierarchy in your household.

Both roles are equally important, yet different. If you're both competing to run your home, you're certain to fail, because you'll find that one of you needs to be the ultimate decision-maker in most situations. Of course, there may occasionally be exceptions to this rule, but for the most part, one of you has to make most of the decisions for the entire family to follow.

When I got married, I was about to graduate from college, and I was young and strong-willed. I was full of knowledge and fully supported the women's liberation movement. I was going to have things my way, which I was convinced was the best way. I even told the person performing the ceremony to take out the vow about obeying my husband, because I was not a dog.

Well, I soon found out that my way was about being stubborn, selfish, strong-willed and spoiled. I found out that this women's lib stuff didn't really work very well. There were no clear-cut roles, no boundaries. Soon, we had a young son, who, of course, noticed there was a lot of yelling going on. Thankfully, we both learned what was going to work and what wasn't, and I slowly began to accept my role as my husband's supporter.

It took some time, because I often thought I knew better. Yet, I began to see that letting my husband make the major decisions helped our household run more smoothly. Once we had several children, there was one person who had the ultimate say, someone no one could argue with.

That meant there was less to fight about, because my husband was setting the major boundaries, and we all followed his lead. Of course, I still had a strong role in the household, especially when he wasn't at home. So I had to make decisions then, but as I got older and wiser, I'd say, "Let's see what your father thinks about this, and then we'll decide."

FIGURING OUT WHAT YOUR ROLE IS

There's so much bad information fed to single people about what their roles should be in a lasting relationship. You're taught that you can have it all. You can be married, have kids, run the household and have a career at the same time. Don't let society tell you what you should do. Be your own person. What they forget to tell you is that doing everything takes a lot of energy. It's really too much for any one person to handle.

Working together is the key. Accepting your role and not stepping on your mate's position is crucial. I admire the single parents that do this well. It's not an easy task at all. If you're a single parent, you have the hardest but most valuable job. If you're lucky enough to be a stay-at-home Mom or Dad, your job is the greatest job of all.

Everyone's heard the saying, "Do what you like" when they're trying to decide what to do with their lives. They say figure out what you like and do that for a living or do it as a side career.

I once heard someone say, "You like to do what you're good at." So simple, but so profound at the same time. I thought about that and realized they were right. I like to plant flowers and put down fresh mulch, because it looks good when I'm done, everyone likes it, and I'm good at it. I like to climb a 12-foot ladder and paint the outside of the house when it needs it. It looks great when I'm done, and I'm good at it. I like the look of freshly vacuumed carpet, so I vacuum often, because I'm good at it.

I'm not good at cooking, though. Therefore, I don't really like to cook. I'd rather buy food someone else has cooked, but I still cook when I have to. If I took some cooking lessons and learned how to make some really tasty dishes, I'd probably start to enjoy cooking. So simple!

What are you good at? Are you good with numbers? Do you enjoy calculating things and writing things down? Maybe you should handle the bill-paying responsibilities for the household, since you're good at it and you enjoy doing it.

Which one of you is good at fixing things, figuring out how things work, or putting things together? That person should do the little repairs around the house, since they're good at it and enjoy it. If your mate is good at cooking, let them cook! If they're good at planning activities, have them be in charge of planning outings and fun times. Different duties work well for different people. Let your mate do what they're good at. Admit that you're not good at everything, and break up the responsibility.

It's important to let your mate fulfill their role in the relationship. Men have an inborn need to lead and be in charge. If you're in a relationship where the man doesn't mind the woman being in charge, you are the exception. If it works and everyone is happy with that arrangement, you're very lucky.

The truth is that most men get their value from the respect they derive being the head of the family and the major decision-maker. The woman's position is just as important, only different. Women are multi-taskers who love to do many things at once. They take on many roles and enjoy each one, but sometimes, they overdo it.

If you tell your mate what to wear, what to like and how to act, you've gone way beyond the boundaries of a healthy relationship. Take a step back and let them make some decisions on their own. The results probably won't be as bad as you think, and it's important that you give them a chance. You're not their mother, after all. You're their mate and supporter.

I've seen this many times. Couples who have obviously been together for a long time, out shopping together. The woman's often telling the man what he should wear, including the style and color he likes. She'll even tell him what size he is, because he doesn't know. Anything the man says he likes, the woman shoots down immediately.

Don't treat your mate like a child. They can make decisions on their own. If they love to wear crazy colors, let them! If they like wearing those bright blue shoes, fine. Let them be themselves.

My husband will often wear unusually long shorts or maybe even a nice pink shirt. He'll joke, "You know, not many people can pull off this look." I always say, "Yes, that's true, but you can." Let your mate express themselves. They'll have fun doing it.

Sacrificial love means not doing what you want to do all the time. Remember the person you fell in love with. Don't try to change them too much. Look at the bigger picture instead of the little things. Be patient and think about what your mate adds to the relationship rather than focusing on the little things that bother you.

Encourage instead of criticizing. Although constructive criticism can at times be beneficial, constant criticism destroys relationships. You should always try to phrase what you say in a nonaggressive way. Constant criticism is a form of control that people use to assume a dominant role.

In order to flow smoothly, the proper hierarchy of the family goes like this: First the husband, then the wife, and then the children. To enjoy true order in the home, it should always fall in that order.

If you put your children above your mate, you're going to have big problems down the road. If the kids see Mom doing the right thing and putting Dad first, they'll learn the proper order of the family and won't be as likely to play you against each other.

Kids only play you against each other when they realize it works. It's fun for them to start some trouble and watch the drama unfold in the house. Once they realize they're in control, they'll use that every chance they get. If you let this go on, you're creating a huge, unnecessary battlefield.

My children never tried to play my husband and me against each other, because they knew the answer they would get. Every time I said, "Dad makes the final decisions. Check with him," that reinforced Dad as the head of the household. They must have heard this a million times.

Make your mate your top priority, the same way you did when you were dating. Your kids will learn some of the greatest lessons in life from watching two strong, happy parents who always back each other up.

While my kids were growing up, I was fortunate to have the opportunity to volunteer at their school a few times a week in addition to working evenings at my nursing job to help with the family expenses. I also helped my husband with his business on Saturdays. My role was always as helper to my husband and mother and caregiver of my children.

Even if you've had your roles out of order for a while, it's never too late to fix that. For the first ten years of our marriage, I was kind of just going with the flow, not really knowing what I was doing. Then I wised up. If you put the roles of the household in their correct order, you'll find great calm and peace. Of course, we had an exception here and there during our kids' teen years, but that's a whole other story. Luckily, my husband stayed pretty firm during those years, so we survived.

WIVES, SUPPORTING YOUR HUSBAND SHOWS GREAT STRENGTH AND RESTRAINT, NOT WEAKNESS

Start redefining those roles today, right now. If you're a woman, begin by showing your mate how much you respect him. Put him at the head of the relationship. Some people love to put this idea in a negative light, like being submissive or what I call being a helper, is something bad.

Actually, your household will be so much more peaceful with this arrangement that there will be little to argue about, which benefits everyone. So don't listen to the masses! You can say the woman's role is submissive and less important, but being supportive is extremely important. It shows great strength and restraint and will help you more than you could ever imagine.

MEN, BEING THE HEAD OF THE HOUSEHOLD MEANS TREATING YOUR WIFE WITH RESPECT

Men, treat your mate with kindness, patience and respect. She is your helpmate. Value her always. Your support of each other will give your relationship great strength and long-term endurance.

Chapter 8
Secrets and Lies

Do you keep secrets from your mate? Do they keep secrets from you? Some things don't need to be discussed, but for some issues, it's critical that they be out in the open. When you were first dating, you didn't share everything. It just seemed unimportant at the time. Did you tell your mate everything about your past relationships? Probably not. Some issues can cause unnecessary pain, so it's best to leave them in the past.

When you were a new couple, you didn't mention every little thing. If your mate's clothes didn't quite match, or their hair was a little messy, you may not have said anything about it. But slowly, you grew more comfortable and began to address those superficial issues. It's the deeper problems that can be tricky.

Does your mate miss work often for no good reason? Party too much? Waste money on silly things? As you grow as a couple, you'll learn it's best to address these issues in a calm, constructive way. Remember that yelling just makes people tune you out. Discussing problems and ways to resolve them will give you the best results.

CHOOSING YOUR WORDS

It's best not to blurt out everything that's on your mind. Choose your words carefully. You can get your point across just as well without being rude and hurtful. Being blatantly honest to the point that you speak harshly to your mate is just mean and hurtful. Be considerate of their feelings. Tell them it's extremely important that the two of you keep things up front. The fewer secrets you keep, the more you'll be able to trust each other.

When I met my husband, I was 20 years old and he was thirty. He admitted some time later that when we first met, he didn't expect us to be together very long due to our age difference. So he decided to have some fun and exaggerate about himself. He told me he owned the small restaurant where he worked, when he was actually a waiter there.

Since I was in college and everyone I knew was a student, I asked him what he was studying. He said he was studying to be a lawyer, when in reality, he hadn't been in school in years. When I told him I liked music, he told me he was a musician, too.

So I went home and told my mother that I'd met this great, mature British guy who owned his own restaurant, was studying to be a lawyer, and was also a musician. She said, "Well, if he's that good, you need to ask his neighbors where he's hiding his wife, because nobody that good is still single!" We still laugh when we remember that now.

If you find out your mate is keeping something from you, address it right away. Find out why they felt they needed to keep it a secret. If it turns out to be a serious issue, you may need to get professional help to deal with it. If you're married, never give up. There's always help available if you want to repair your relationship. If you're dealing with physical abuse, that's the extreme situation. Get help outside the home as soon as possible.

If your mate has been unfaithful, you might think you can't forgive them or ever move past it. Yet even this type of betrayal can be healed in time if you're willing to put in the effort together. Always attempt to repair the relationship if possible. After you've calmed down, try to find a good counselor and devote a significant amount of attention to the issues you need to address. It takes two to make a relationship work, and both of you will need to work together.

After you've met with a counselor, you'll be more prepared to decide whether you can save your relationship or not. Don't make this decision until you've put some serious time and effort into working things out. Unfortunately, there will always be those extreme cases where your mate may choose not to change their ways, and that's not your fault. If that's the case, do your best to slowly pick up the pieces and move on with your life.

SECRETS ARE REALLY ABOUT PAINFUL ISSUES

Does your mate spend money like it grows on trees? Why do they feel the need to do that? If they buy things to make themselves feel better, talk to them and get to the root of their unhappiness. If they want to treat themselves to something special once in a while, that's fine as long as you can afford it.

But if their spending has gotten out of control, they may need help. There are support groups available for every addiction you can think of, from overeating to gambling. Get information about the free support groups available in your area and go with your mate to a meeting. Don't just get upset with them and leave them to work it out all alone. Offer your support and get involved.

Often, people know that help is available, but won't take that first step to reach out for it. If your mate won't go to a meeting, go yourself so you can learn about the real underlying causes behind their addiction. Just don't give up! You can help your mate by understanding their problem more deeply, even if they don't understand it themselves. Secrets are quiet for a reason; they cause pain. Most of us don't like to deal with painful issues.

If you're keeping a secret from your mate, they probably already know something about it. If you've been together for a while, they probably know you better than you know yourself, and they know something's not right. They probably noticed changes in your behavior before you were even aware there was a serious problem.

Be honest with them. Your actions affect both of you. You'd be wise to seek out their help. Don't let pride keep you from having a trusting relationship. Admit when you've done something wrong, and ask for help correcting it.

It may take some time, but eventually you'll get to the point that you'll be able to talk about just about anything with your mate. It took my husband and me many years to let our guard down enough to talk about things we didn't want to discuss from our past – difficulties and experiences we'd gone through during our dating years, before we met.

Now we're at the point where we just talk about anything and can laugh about it. You can choose to learn from your difficulties and turn them into something positive. This is good for both of you. Secrets are really about underlying issues that need to be dealt with. A strong couple that wants to work things out can overcome the most difficult problems together.

You've probably heard about the seven-year itch. This happens when people start to get bored in their relationship and maybe act out of character. I've heard about it, but thankfully, my husband and I never experienced it. We pretty much act toward each other the same way we did when we first met. No big secrets, no major issues left unaddressed, no question about how we feel about each other, just a continuation of the fun we've always had together.

When people say it's hard to be married, I just look at them and think, *Wow, it's really so simple.* Yet people continually make it so difficult. I don't understand why. Many choose not to use the tools and techniques they need to make their relationship work. Others just really don't want to make the effort. Some simply refuse to change their selfish ways.

It's so much easier to do things the right way the first time than to do them wrong and then try to fix things. So keep things up front with no big secrets. Let go of the weight that all of those lies and inconsistencies have been putting on your back. The truth is freeing and makes life so much lighter and more peaceful. Just try it and see for yourself!

Chapter 9
Date Nights, Snuggling and Intimacy

Do you still go out on dates with your mate? You know how much fun it is to spend an exciting evening out on the town. Earlier in the book, we talked about our dating days, when going out was something special we looked forward to all week. Remember how creative you were when planning a big night out?

As a teen, I remember spending nights out lying on wet grass on the hills of the golf course, looking up at the moon and smooching my date under the stars. Then there were the evenings spent at some school or park, playing on the playground with my date, happily chatting and getting to know one another.

I remember driving half an hour to the beach on a Friday night and playing in the ocean all evening with my date. We'd end up completely soaked and spend the whole drive home laughing and smiling about our night out. Of course, there was also the ever-popular snuggling in the car. This usually happened in the park, at the mall, outside a club, or in the driveway. It didn't matter where we were. It was just so much fun.

I remember one late evening, I was kissing a boy in his car, which was parked outside of an elementary school. Then suddenly, a police officer walked up, shone his flashlight on us and asked, "What are you two doing?" My date said, "Having a midnight rendezvous," to which the officer replied, "Go have your midnight rendezvous somewhere else." Those days were so much fun.

Back then, you made the effort to make the evening memorable, whether you were going to the movies, a football game, a restaurant, or maybe even a play. You went out of your way to take yourselves out of the daily routine. You were able to escape from all of your responsibilities, even if it was just for an evening. Do you remember how much fun that was? I don't think that you do. If you did, you'd still be doing it!

MAKE AN EFFORT TO HAVE FUN!

Let's start with something easy to get your relationship back on track. My husband and I have always been snugglers. When our children were growing up, we always sat next to each other on the couch, leaning toward each other, side by side. He'd be watching the news, and I'd be reading something. I'd always be sitting close to him. He'd be watching a football game, and I'd be making some jewelry at his side. It's always been this way.

Do you snuggle on the couch, or do you have separate recliners? That's fine sometimes, but try to make the effort to sit close together at the end of the day, just to spend some quiet time together.

How often do the two of you go out for a date night? You might think it's too hard, especially if you have children. At the end of the week, you may think, "I'm too tired from work. It's just easier to stay home." Some people say, "I just can't afford to go out and spend a lot of money."

Well, first of all, if you have kids, there's always a babysitter to be found. Ask a grandparent, a sister, a friend. Trade babysitting evenings with someone you know who also has young children. Do whatever you have to do to find someone!

You say you're too tired to go out with your mate? Can you still walk? Then you're not so tired that you can't make some effort to go out and have a good time. Think you can't afford to go out? There are so many inexpensive options out there. Take a stroll along the beach or a nearby lake. Attend a free concert in the park. When you were young, you didn't have any money, yet you still found inexpensive ways to have a good time. Put some thought into new ways to have fun.

My husband and I go to the movies every week, or at least every other week. We also enjoy a good concert a few times each year, and we go out to lunch together whenever our schedules permit. We aim for weekly lunches, and go out for ice cream in the evening whenever we can. We just sit and chat at the tables outside. When we have a day off together, we go to museums. In other words, we think of ways to have special time together, and then we actually do it, not just talk about it.

You might say, "I love to go to the theatre and see a good play or the ballet, but there's no way my mate would ever go." Well, if you promise him some extra special fun in the romance department afterwards, I promise he'll go. He'll be in a hurry to go. He'll be asking, "When's the next play?"

ROMANCE DOESN'T HAVE TO FADE AWAY

Do you still hold hands? Do you put your arms around each other when you're out? Do you still kiss in the car, or have you become more like roommates? Keeping the romance alive takes effort, but not as much as you might think. How easy it is to start kissing your mate in the car, the parking lot, or just while walking down the sidewalk. My husband and I always joke when we get carried away somewhere, "I hope this doesn't end up on YouTube!"

It doesn't take much to get the mood going. Do you make an effort to wear something your mate likes? Sometimes, that's all you need to get the mood going in the right direction. Get rid of that old tee shirt. If you're a woman, slap on some makeup and dig out those sexy heels or boots. You don't have to overdo this.

Guys, I know you love that beer t-shirt you've been wearing for years, but how about wearing something that buttons down? Men and women are both visual. Get dressed up when you go out to do something exciting, to help set the mood.

Try something you haven't done in a while. Haven't made out at the lake or beach since you were a teen? Do it! Why do many people have affairs? There are many reasons, but mainly because couples stop doing the things they did when they were first together, and someone comes along that helps them relive their youth and feel alive again. If this were happening with their own mate, they probably wouldn't even think of going elsewhere. Meet that need in your mate, so someone else doesn't.

You had no problem keeping your relationship exciting in your early days. When you were young and had a tough week and someone special asked you out, did you say, "No, I'm too tired?" Heck, no, you didn't! Stop acting like you're 90 years old! If you're still walking, you've got the energy to spice up your relationship.

You might say, well, we've been like this for a while. It's too late or too hard to change now. That's nonsense! That just says you're not willing to make the effort to make your mate happy, or yourself, either. Remember what we said before? When you say, "I can't," what you really mean is "I won't."

PEOPLE DON'T REALLY CHANGE

My wonderful mother-in-law was a funny English woman who loved to tell a good joke. I remember during the early years of our marriage, she asked me, "Do you know when men are ready to stop having sex?"

I said, "When?"

"After they've been in the grave two weeks!" she laughed.

I laughed back then without realizing what that really meant. Now I know it means that men don't change, and women don't really change, either. Even as we get older and a bit wrinkled on the outside, we still have a 20-year-old on the inside that's dying to come out and have some fun.

One late evening while I was at work, I noticed that one of my older patients, a petite lady in her early nineties, was still awake. When I entered her room, I saw she had a small light on and was curled up under a blanket, reading a book. When I asked why she was up so late, she said, "Oh, I was just reading the most wonderful book. It's a romantic story about a young couple who are deeply in love." She smiled and looked at me, and I realized that behind that gray hair and wrinkled eyes, a dreamy young girl still lived inside.

We really don't change that much as we get older. Take care of your mate's needs. The longer you're together, the more you should want to spoil them for continuing to care for you and love you unconditionally for so long.

Men, pamper your mate with flowers, small gifts, or a note telling her how you feel about her. These things keep the romance alive and show her that you're thinking of her.

Ladies, the next time you're at the mall, step into the lingerie shop. No, I'm not talking about the shop with the "5 for $10" underwear sign. I'm talking about the one with the fun stuff. Go inside and get yourself an outfit. Actually, get a couple. You don't have to have a perfect figure. Anyone can improve their appearance with some nice lingerie. And no flannel PJ's, either! It takes very little effort to do something like this, but you'll reap all the benefits if you do.

Do you often have a headache when your sweetheart wants to snuggle? Take some Tylenol and stop with the rejecting. Once in a while is understandable, but all the time is discouraging. Are you doing the same old thing in the bedroom that you've been doing for years? Or maybe, you're doing very little at all. If so, you'd better spice it up. The responsibility falls on both people. If it's been a while, you may have to take the initiative.

Don't wait too long between your romantic interludes. You should abstain no longer than a short time that's mutually agreed upon. That's right, I said *mutually* agreed upon. For most men, that will be a short time. I'll explain later where I first heard about this agreement. If two people are making at least half an effort, no matter how tired you are, you should be having a pretty good time.

Boring sex? Those two words don't even go together. If you're making even a little effort, you will not be bored. You'll be so glad you did, and your mate will, too. Everyone will notice your quiet, happy contentment and those permanent smiles on your faces. Only the two of you will know the secret behind those smiles.

If your physical relationship is not a priority, you don't know much about men or women. They say respect is a man's number one need, and intimacy is second. In my experience, I'd say that both issues are fighting for that number one spot. Don't neglect this aspect of your relationship. You don't want your mate looking for that type of attention somewhere else. If your mate is happy, they'll make you happy in return.

So go ahead and get some slinky lingerie. Plan an evening of creative intimacy. Check into a cheap motel for some alone time. Have that makeout session in the car. Whatever you have to do, do it.

It's not rocket science. Both people need to put in the effort to make the romance happen.

It doesn't matter who starts this change. If you return your relationship to its early days, you'll rekindle the fire you may have lost and return it to the forefront of your relationship. And you'll have those stars in your eyes once again!

Chapter 10
Drifting Apart

Have you been a couple for a while, and consistently drifting apart in your relationship? It seems like many couples let themselves fall into this trap. Your priorities might include a job that requires long hours. If you're a parent, your priority might be giving all of your time and attention to your kids. If you have a lot of family and friends, or are very involved in the community, your priority might lie in activities outside the home. If you like to have the last word in every discussion and always have to be right, maybe your priority is yourself.

The only way to avoid drifting apart is to make your relationship with your mate your top priority. You can't work 70-80 hours a week and not expect your relationship to suffer. Do you really have enough energy to work all of those hours and pay sufficient attention to your mate, too? Probably not. Most of us have to work, but to keep your relationship strong, you'll need to keep your work schedule reasonable.

Do you put all of your energy into your kids and their activities, and then collapse into bed at the end of each day? Be honest. Do your kids really need to participate in all of those activities? Maybe you need to narrow it down to just one or two of their favorites. Back in the day, kids were happy just playing outside and not being pulled from one activity to another after school.

Do you spend a lot of time doing things for family and friends? That's great, as long as it doesn't keep you from paying attention to your mate. If it drains all of your energy, it's going to be a problem. Try to keep your time away limited to a reasonable amount. If possible, schedule this while your mate is at work or away so as not to cut into your time together.

Are you super-involved in the community and in charge of every club? Again, you really don't need to be the soccer mom, the dance mom, the karate mom, the football and baseball mom and the PTA mom. Narrow it down! Don't try to convince your mate that all of those activities are really necessary. He'll just shake his head.

The same goes for men who've drifted away from their mates. They're out with their buddies, watching football games and going fishing or hunting. None of these things in and of themselves is wrong, if done once in a while. It's only a problem if it's making you and your mate lead separate lives.

If you've been a couple for a while, do you still have common interests? Or do you each do your own thing and act more like roommates? Do you get annoyed with each other easily and often? Drifting apart is a process.

Do you tend to look at things through your own eyes and not from your mate's perspective? Do you need to be right all of the time? Are you rude to them? Do you have to have the last word whenever you disagree? The reason for this is simple. You've become selfish and self-centered over time. You basically want things your own way.

You can't make a relationship work long-term if you keep putting yourself first. Some people will tolerate it, but it makes everything in your life so much more difficult. Even if they put up with it, your mate will not be happy about it.

I see people who have drifted apart all the time. She does her own thing, and he does his. She spends all of her time with her girlfriends shopping or does everything with her kids. Sometimes, you can't even tell these people have a spouse!

And if you're teaching this pattern to your kids, it's a huge problem, one they're sadly likely to pass on to the next generation.

DON'T PASS BAD PATTERNS ONTO YOUR KIDS!

If your kids don't see their parents fussing over each other, making time for each other and making their relationship a priority, they won't know how to do it themselves. They'll most likely display this same learned behavior when they begin having their own adult relationships. The apple doesn't fall far from the tree.

Why is divorce so prevalent? People drift apart for one simple reason. They haven't kept their relationship with their mate as a top priority. They don't use the tools needed to keep a long-term relationship going.

My husband and I have another unspoken rule. Again, we never discussed it. It was just understood. We've never allowed ourselves to use the "D" word, as we called it. We completely removed the word "divorce" from our vocabulary. It has never been spoken in our house.

If you decide early on that divorce is a subject you'll never bring up, then it's easy to realize it's never going to be a topic of discussion. If you're the type of person who throws this word around freely, you're asking for trouble. Your mate has their limits on how often they'll tolerate having that thrown in their face.

If things are really ugly and there's a lot of yelling going on, you'll have to make a decision to start acting more maturely and stop trying to resolve things that way. Contrary to popular opinion, loud doesn't equal right. I know a lot of people think that way. They yell and yell and yell until the whole neighborhood knows what's going on. Get a hold of yourselves.

I THINK I HAVE MADE A MISTAKE

I know a lot of people who are now divorced and older who've realized in hindsight that their spouse wasn't really that bad. Unfortunately, now, it's too late. Their spouse has remarried, and now all the available men and women have a lot of baggage to go along with them.

If you're divorced and meet a great man or woman, you should ask yourself why they're still available. Maybe they also think they're a great catch and they're holding out for the perfect person. If so, your options are even more limited than you might have expected. Often, divorced people end up being alone. They'll be the first to tell you that they made a mistake and urge you not to do the same.

If you're the one who tried to make it work with no positive results and put up with affairs or even physical abuse, don't be too hard on yourself. Some people will never change. Try to pick up the pieces as best you can. If you have children, try to keep things as peaceful as possible for both the children's sake and your own.

If you're part of a couple that has broken up, you may have already found that the grass is not really greener on the other side. If your mate hasn't moved on yet, let them know you've made a mistake. Give them all of the time in the world to reconsider trying again.

Maybe you've been drifting apart for years. If so, it will take some time to rebuild your relationship, but remember that it can be done. You hear about people splitting up and going their own way for a while, maybe even trying other relationships, only to return to their mate in the end. It's a shame so many people have to get hurt in the process.

Many relationships can be rebuilt if both people take responsibility for their relationship getting off track. Apart from abuse or infidelity, divorce is usually just selfish, plain and simple. People think, "I want things my way or no way." This is an adult tantrum that goes on and on. Both sides can be equally selfish if neither person is willing to budge to make things better.

Think about one of those old couples you've seen holding hands. Why have they lasted so long? They didn't fall for the selfish ways that are pushed down our throats from every direction in society.

You can be that middle-aged divorced woman hitting the clubs, looking for Mr. Perfect. Only there is no Mister Perfect. What you're looking for doesn't actually exist.

You can be that older man trying to recapture your youth with a younger woman. Well, you'd better be careful. What are her motives? You'd better be sure they're genuine and not self-seeking.

My husband and I always joke about what a nightmare it would be to have to start dating again at our age. It was hard enough when we were young! I can't imagine how much more difficult it must be once you're older.

The best thing I can tell you if you've drifted apart and see only a slight chance of saving your relationship? Grab it. If you've been together for a while, you have more in common than you realize, and a history together that can never be erased. No one can replace the time and emotional investment you've put into your long-term relationship. This relationship will always be in the back of your mind. So choose to save it. Start each day by making a little effort to slowly come back together. Build on that little hope, one small step at a time.

Chapter 11
Left for Last – The Best-Kept Secret

At last! I always leave the best part of a story for last. Now I'll share how all of these issues and simple solutions can be found in one manual that is proven to be perfectly correct. Some of you may already know that you'll find all of these questions and their answers in the Bible.

That's right. God gave us our existence. He created us and knows exactly what our needs and wants are, before we even understand them. As 2 Timothy 3:16 states, *All Scripture is inspired by God and is useful to teach us what is true and to make us realize what is wrong in our lives.*

God made Man. He tells us what Man's needs, desires and issues are. God made Woman from a man. She is different and has different wants and needs than a man.

You can find out everything about men and women and how they are in this one book! You might be thinking, "I've tried to read the Bible, but it's just too hard to understand." Well, there are now many versions that have been accurately translated into modern language. You can read these Bibles as easily as one of today's popular novels. I'll include verses in this chapter from one of the newer translations, the New Living Translation (NLT).

Let's start with seeing what the Bible has to say about being in love. Our thoughts are so magical and dreamy when we first realize we've fallen in love. The first chapter of the Song of Solomon reads, "*Kiss me and kiss me again, for your love is sweeter than wine..."* (Song of Solomon 1:2)

This poetic song captures the intensity of new love, saying, *"My lover is mine and I am his...* (Song of Solomon 2:16) and *"You have captured my heart, my treasure..."* (Song of Solomon 4:9)

We're in another world, daydreaming about love, when we first experience it. We can't think of anything else but our beloved. Our perspective is altered, so we view our mate through rose-colored glasses. Life is wonderful.

Our hearts are so delicate. *Guard your heart above all else, for it determines the course of your life.* (Proverbs 4:23) Everything we feel when we're newly in love seems to come from our heart, and every emotion is so magnified. We feel everything so deeply. That's why we must guard our heart so closely at this time. It's best not to become involved in relationships that we're not yet equipped to handle emotionally while you're young, because you may not be fully mature yet.

Many of us are not yet ready to deal with the issues that come with having a close adult relationship at this young age. So slow it down during your dating years and enjoy the innocence of your youth. Don't be in such a hurry to have a grown-up relationship! They're complicated, and you haven't yet developed the tools to make them work, so keep them light and playful. Enjoy the sweetness of your youth. The Bible says young people should be busy "*singing psalms and hymns and spiritual songs among yourselves and making music to the Lord in your hearts.*" (Ephesians 5:19)

Respect and Communication

Love is patient, love is kind. Love is not jealous or boastful or proud or rude. It does not demand its own way. It is not irritable, and it keeps no record of being wronged. (1 Corinthians 13:4-5)

Learning how to communicate and respect your mate is one of the biggest foundations of your relationship. It's important for you to learn how to speak calmly and kindly to your mate all of the time, not just when you feel like it.

In other words, don't be bossy or talk down to your mate. You are not better than them. Don't act like a spoiled child if you don't get your way every time.

He who restrains his lips is wise. (Proverbs 10:19) *People who wink at wrong cause trouble...* (Proverbs 10:10) *The lips of the godly speak helpful words..."* (Proverbs 10:32)

Let go of things that happened yesterday, last week, and last year. This will allow you to express true, unconditional love in its purest form. Pride causes so much conflict in relationships. If you can swallow your pride, stay humble and put your mate before yourself, you'll start to see a new light blossom around your relationship. *Pride leads to disgrace, but with humility comes wisdom.* (Proverbs 11:2) *People who accept discipline are on the pathway to life...* (Proverbs 10:17)

In other words, when we're prideful, we later feel ashamed because we behaved so badly. When we remain humble and calm, we gain so much, because we cause fewer problems for ourselves. Be willing to change, and your wisdom will grow.

Appearance – Working with What You Have

You are beautiful, my darling, beautiful beyond words. Your eyes are like doves behind your veil. (Song of Solomon 4:1) *You are so handsome, my love, pleasing beyond words!* (Song of Solomon 1:16) *She makes her own bedspreads. She dresses in fine linen and purple gowns.* (Proverbs 31:22)

Do you remember the first time you saw your mate? I remember exactly how my husband looked, right down to the blue jeans and fitted, striped short-sleeved shirt he was wearing. That image is frozen in my mind. In fact, I still have that shirt more than 28 years later.

Before he ever said a word, I was taken with his blue eyes, blond hair, and the way he smiled when he laughed. I was immediately smitten. I'm sure you have a similar recollection of your mate's appearance when you first met.

Our vision is what first attracts us to each other, and our physical appearance continues to be an important aspect of any long-term relationship. If you've been together for a while, you might think that it doesn't matter how you look anymore, but it does.

You don't have to be perfect, because your mate already loves you for who you are. But if you dress up a bit or do a little something special with your appearance, it shows that you care about their needs. Being a perfect size or shape is not the goal. Just enhancing your look is really all you need to do.

Sometimes, I wake up in the morning, look in the mirror, and say, "Yikes! Who is *that*?" Then, I start the process of fixing myself up. Your mate will appreciate any effort you make, however small, because they'll know you're doing it for them.

You don't have to overdo it. Your goal is simply to please *your* mate, not everyone else's mate! No need to go overboard! Looking stylish doesn't mean dressing inappropriately. A nice new outfit or fresh haircut may be all that you need. In fact, if this is the worst problem in your relationship, consider yourself lucky! Remember that? Because something so simple can be fixed in less than a day with just a bit of shopping. So go out and treat yourself to something new and have some fun. It's a win-win situation. You get to enjoy a new look that pleases your mate as well.

Of course, some people are quite beautiful on the outside, but need to work on their inner selves. We all know some that are beautiful on the inside, but have let their outer appearance go. Anyone can be beautiful, both inside and out!

If you need to lose weight due to health concerns, get help before you develop a permanent health issue. Weight Watchers is within everyone's budget. Even some weight loss physicians have lowered their fees. You may find that you do best in a program that requires weekly accountability. Don't put it off. Start feeling better today.

Beneficial Friendships and Dealing with the Past

The heartfelt counsel of a friend is as sweet as perfume and incense. (Proverbs 27:9) *A friend is always loyal...* (Proverbs 17:17). *There are friends who destroy each other, but a real friend sticks closer than a brother.* (Proverbs 18:24)

Friends and family are one of the biggest treasures of this life. Your friends are there to lift you up when you need it, and family's there to remind you that you'll never have to deal with anything alone. They're your support, no matter what. My family is large and very close. They're also the kings and queens of storytelling, so they're great fun as well.

I'm also fortunate enough to have friends who are like family. Some I have known most of my life. My friends have been there to correct me whenever I did something stupid. They cried with me when I went through difficult times. They even laughed with me when we realized much later how comical many of our "crises" actually were.

Now, let's go back a bit. It's always fun to remember and reminisce about our dating days. They were just so much fun. We all remember being crazy about particular boys and girls. Of course, we can't forget the emotional roller coaster ride that we were on at that time.

I thought every boy I dated was awesome, and I never wanted any of those relationships to end. Whether it was a few weeks, a couple of months, or a longer time, I almost always cried like a baby when it was over, even when I knew it was time to move on.

Luckily, I learned great lessons during my dating years that greatly prepared me for the relationship I would have with my husband. Whenever I did something wrong, like maybe not treating a boy as well as I should have during those days, it always seemed to come back to bite me later on. Of course, it felt much worse when I was the one feeling the pain instead of them.

Don't be misled. You cannot mock the justice of God. You will always harvest what you plant. (Galatians 6:7)

That's right. You always reap what you sow. My girlfriends tease me about how I was the crybaby of the group. And though I cried, now I'm so grateful for the lessons I learned. They taught me about the boundaries we have to maintain in order to make our relationship work. So for me, those years were priceless.

Some of you have to stay connected to previous relationships if you have children together. Always remember to keep the peace for the children's sake, and to show respect for all of the adults involved. No yelling, no name calling, and no insulting the new spouse or your past mate.

Children watch you and learn from everything you do, far more than what you say. Remember that they didn't ask to be put into this situation. So put their needs first. Be the bigger person if necessary.

The following verses are probably my favorites. *But to you who are willing to listen, I say, love your enemies. Do good to those who hate you. Bless those who curse you. Pray for those who hurt you.* (Luke 6:27-28) *If you love only those who love you, why should you get credit for that? Even sinners love those who love them! And if you do good only to those who do good to you, why should you get credit? Even sinners do that much!* (Luke 6:32-33)

By being kind to those who are not kind to you, you're showing true obedience to God. God loves everyone. Follow His example, and you'll be rewarded in so many ways!

Fighting Constructively

Do you like to stir things up, just to get a little reaction out of your mate? If you're young, this is typical. But if you're mature, you should realize that this is childish and destructive. *When I was a child, I spoke and thought and reasoned as a child. But when I grew up, I put away childish things.* (1 Corinthians 13:11)

You really don't have to fight. It's a choice. I used to scream, yell and fight to get my own way, but I learned that that type of behavior destroys your mate's enthusiasm for your relationship, and it tears them down. Build your mate up instead. And don't use foul or abusive language. *Let everything you say be good and helpful, so that your words will be an encouragement to those who hear them.* (Ephesians 4:29) *Get rid of all bitterness, rage, anger, harsh words and slander as well as all types of evil behavior.* (Ephesians 4:31)

And "don't sin by letting anger control you." Don't let the sun go down while you are still angry..." (Ephesians 4:26) God says to make up with your mate before the sun goes down when you're angry. If you do this even sooner, you'll waste less time being upset with each other.

Our pride almost always gets us in trouble. This problem is so old that it goes back to a time when the most beautiful angel created by God, Lucifer, rebelled against Him, because he wanted to be higher than God. *How you are fallen from heaven, o shining star, son of the morning! You have been thrown down to the earth, you who have destroyed the nations of the world! For you said to yourself, I will ascend to heaven, and set my throne above God's stars.* (Isaiah 14:12-13)

I can't even tell you how dumb that was. Yes, even angels that were created before Man had a problem with pride. And they were all male. There are no female angels mentioned in the Bible. The angels existed before Man.

Many believe that if you know the Lord, you'll become an angel when you die, but this is not stated in the Bible. Those who believe in Christ are actually known as the saints of the church age, not future angels.

So the issue of pride has been around forever and is in fact, one of the original sins. Pride can destroy not only your relationship, but entire nations. That's how devastatingly powerful pride can be. Be aware of your prideful feelings on a daily basis, and choose to behave differently.

Experts say it takes 21 days to form a new habit. This one may take longer, but it can be done. With it will come flowing benefits that trickle down to every aspect of your relationship. Smart small. You'll get better at it as you go. *We destroy every proud obstacle that keeps people from knowing God."* (2 Corinthians 10:5)

If you're in counseling with your mate and it's working, I can guarantee the concepts being used probably came straight from the Bible. If it's not working, even though you're both doing your part, you're probably not getting the right advice. Remember that you don't need the advice of the world. Man is fallible. He makes mistakes. Never follow Man's advice over God's!

Managing Finances

How is your financial situation? Money problems are the number one cause of divorce, so it's critical that you get this part of your relationship under control. Nobody's perfect, but there are many boundaries you can stay within to keep your head above water, even if your income is not that high. Do you use credit cards a lot? If you can pay them off each month, then it's not a problem. If not, you're creating a heavy burden that could be hanging over your head for a while.

Just as the rich rule the poor, so the borrower is servant to the lender. (Proverbs 22:7) If you owe on things that are not necessities and can't pay for them in a timely manner, you have become the servant to the lender. They now have the control. If you took the bait, like we all have, they're holding the line and we have to repay what we've spent. Try not to live off of your credit cards. I'm pretty sure that if we looked back at the majority of the items we've purchased on those credit cards, we'd have to admit that few were things we truly needed.

There are over 1,000 verses on possessions and finances in the Bible. That tells you what a huge problem this is for Man. *No one can serve two masters. For you will hate one and love the other.* (Matthew 6:24) *Do not lay up your treasures on earth, where moth and rust destroy, where thieves break in and steal.* (Matthew 6:19) *Trust in your money and down you go.* (Proverbs 11:28). If you put all of your trust in material things, you will eventually fall.

Focusing on money instead of the real gifts of this life will leave you with nothing but emptiness. Money cannot buy love, joy or true friendship. You may be more comfortable for a while, but at the end of the day, if you don't have true riches, the emptiness will still be there. *Carefully determine what pleases the Lord.* (Ecclesiastes 5:10)

Learn to be happy with your circumstances rather than your possessions. Remember that it's not the amount of money coming in that makes you content. It's the amount going out which you can successfully manage that helps you obtain true peace.

Never try to get ahead by hurting someone else. *Wealth gained by get-rich-quick schemes quickly disappears; wealth from hard work grows over time.* (Proverbs 13:11) When you do something wrong to someone else in order to get ahead, or for any reason, you reap what you sow. It always comes back to bite you, eventually. Wealth grows over time through hard work. In most cases, the harder you work, the more you will get paid.

If you're in the midst of a financial crisis, try to correct it, one step at a time. Take each day one day at a time. Don't worry about what might happen in the future; you're not there yet. *So don't worry about tomorrow, for tomorrow will bring its own worries. Today's trouble is enough for today.* (Matthew 6:34)

Can all your worries add a single moment to your life? (Matthew 6:27) Of course not, so begin today. Start shopping at that discount store. Take a peek at that clearance rack. Go to that small family grocer where you can save a bundle. Maybe trade in that fancy new car for a beautiful used car. Pay cash as often as possible. The list of ways to save money is endless. You just have to make the choice to do it. You put yourself in this situation, so you can make the changes to get yourself out, one step at a time.

Roles and Responsibilities

Is the order of your household somewhat confusing? Do the kids run your household, or do the parents? Does the woman make all of the decisions, leaving the man wondering what he's supposed to do?

Most of us don't really know how to make the household run smoothly. Many mothers are so devoted to their children that they forget about their mate's needs. If a man doesn't feel needed and important in a relationship, he'll turn to other things to fill that need. Women will do the same if they don't feel valued.

Put your house in order this way: God first, as the ultimate authority who knows how to do everything best. The man's position is second. *For wives, this means submit to your husbands as to the Lord. For a husband is the head of his wife as Christ is head of the church.* (Ephesians 5:22-23)

Again ladies, submitting doesn't mean becoming a mere shadow of yourself. It takes great strength and discipline for a woman to let her mate fulfill his role and accept his inborn need to lead. *Then the Lord God said, "It is not good for the man to be alone. I will make him a helper who is just right for him."* (Genesis 2:18)

Two people are better than one, for they can help each other succeed. (Ecclesiastes 4:9)... *a triple braided cord is not easily broken.* (Ecclesiastes 4:12)

It's still the man's responsibility to value the woman as much as he values himself. *Husbands, love your wives and never treat them harshly.* (Colossians 3:19) If you're a woman and you've been running the relationship for a while, let your mate start making some of the decisions. You'll see a new strength and contentment begin to lift up your mate in his new role.

Secrets and Lies

Do your battles include secrets, lies and shameful activities? A relationship without trust is doomed to fail. And keeping things from your mate takes more effort than just being truthful. You inflict unnecessary pain on them by lying and doing things behind their back. *All day long, you plot destruction. Your tongue cuts like a sharp razor; you're an expert at telling lies.* (Psalm 52:2)

Putting confidence in an unreliable person in times of trouble is like chewing with a broken tooth or walking on a lame foot. (Proverbs 25:19) Are you so selfish that you don't mind putting the one you say you love through great pain? Your mate knows deep down when you are being deceitful. You're not fooling anyone. *Smooth words may hide a wicked heart, just as a pretty glaze covers a clay pot.* (Proverbs 26:23)

Leading a shameful life causes more pain than dealing with any underlying issues that need to be addressed. Put your mate and your family before yourself. Start being more truthful, one day at a time. *Trustworthy messengers refresh like snow in summer.* (Proverbs 25:13) It's up to you. If you want your relationship to survive, start being honest today.

Date Nights, Snuggling and Intimacy

Do you spend enough time snuggling with your mate, or are you too tired, too busy, or just not that interested? Intimacy between a man and a woman was created by God and meant to continue as an important part of their union. *The husband should fulfill his wife's sexual needs, and the wife should fulfill the husband's needs.* (I Corinthians 7:3)

Give honor to marriage and remain faithful to one another in marriage. (Hebrews 13:4) The marriage bed cannot be defiled. If your bedroom has become boring and uneventful, you need to get creative and get busy! You're not supposed to neglect this aspect of your relationship. *Do not deprive each other of sexual relations unless you both agree to refrain from sexual intimacy for a limited time so you can give yourselves more completely to prayer.* (I Corinthians 7:5)

Did you read that part about "a limited time?" I learned this lesson about sixteen years ago in my ladies' Bible Study when we did a study on marriage. This had a huge effect on me, as I realized that most people, even those in the church, don't follow this command. If they did, there would be a lot more men whistling as they work and women with permanent smiles on their faces!

To keep your mate content and avoid temptation to wander or look to something else to fill this need, you need to put great importance on this aspect of your relationship. *Drink water from your own well...* (Proverbs 5:15)

That's right. You want your mate to drink water from his own well, not look for something or someone else to quench that thirst. Men and women both have this responsibility to care for their mate intimately.

Have you been a couple for a while and need to rekindle the romance? ... *Rejoice in the wife of your youth.* (Proverbs 5:18) When I was younger, I didn't fully understand what that meant. I wondered, "Once you're old, how can you enjoy your mate the same way you did when you were young?"

But now that I'm older, I get it. I still see my husband the same way I did when we were young. He looks no different to me now than he did back then, because I still have those rose-colored glasses on. We still date each other. So go back to the time when your relationship was magical, and bring those special feelings back.

Drifting Apart

Have the two of you been drifting apart for years, or have you considered leaving your spouse? If you're looking for greener pastures when you haven't been watering your own grass, don't expect different results. *The person who stays away from common sense will end up in the company of the dead.* (Proverbs 21:16)

Look at the couples who get along well and whose relationships have lasted long-term. Ask them for advice on how they've made it work. Whether they realize it or not, they've probably been using God-given techniques to keep their relationships going strong.

Human plans, no matter how well-devised, cannot stand against the Lord. So don't listen to what society tells you about how you should feel or how you should manage your relationship. *So we must listen very carefully to the truth we have heard, or we may drift away from it.* (Hebrews 2:1)

Give your relationship the attention it needs. Do you pay more attention to your kids, your job or your social life than your mate? Be wise and focus on rebuilding your relationship. Piece it back together so you don't risk ending up alone. *Whoever pursues righteousness and unfailing love will find life, righteousness and honor.* (Proverbs 21:21)

The Best-Kept Secret

In our house, we choose to worship the God of the Bible, our Lord Jesus Christ. His teachings are the oldest historically-documented faith still in existence today. That's right. That means that all of the other major religions of our time came *after* the early Old Testament writings.

Christianity is also the **only** religion whose biblical prophecy has been fulfilled over and over. No other religion has the detailed predictions that have come true every time like the Bible does. Events that were predicted thousands of years before they occurred have come true every single time. And some of the most interesting events are still to come! I hope you'll take the time to think about what that really means.

I'm sure some people will disagree with some of the ideas I've written about. Some may disagree with a lot of them. That's fine. I'm just sharing what has worked for me and my husband and sharing the source of the teachings that have served us so well in our relationship.

Take as little or as much as you like from these timeless scriptures and their meaning. If you've lost faith in God, look to the God who created the universe. Does anyone else have that kind of knowledge and understanding with such precise order? Can the one you worship create galaxies? I didn't think so.

Man has been able to do amazing things with the knowledge that God has allowed to be revealed to him, but he hasn't come close to creating the sun, the moon, the atmosphere, and the precise conditions needed for all of these things to exist. Not even close.

So stop looking to Man for answers. Man is fallible. He makes mistakes. *For as the heavens are higher than the earth, so my ways are higher than your ways and my thoughts higher than your thoughts.* (Isaiah 55:9) Pray to the Lord Jesus for the answers you seek.

In the beginning, the Word already existed. The Word was with God, and the Word was God... So the Word became human and made his home among us. (John 1:1, 14) Jesus said, "*I and the Father are one.*" (John 10:30)

That's right. There is only one God, with three persons in the Godhead. You reject one, and you reject them all.

Jesus also said, "*... Anyone who has seen me has seen the Father. So why are you asking to see Him? Don't you believe that I am in the*

Father and the Father is in me?" (John 14:9, 10)

Trying to understand the trinity of God is complex and beyond complete understanding. My way to attempt to understand this is that just as a man can be a father and a son and also have a spiritual aspect of himself all at the same time, God does as well. He is father, son and spirit all at once, each aspect being equally important but separate, with each having a unique purpose and way of teaching. Yet God can be omnipresent, in more than one place at once, where Man can't. *For there is no other God but me, a righteous God and Savior. There is none but Me.* (Isaiah 45:21)

I get upset when people say that God sends people to Hell. No, people send themselves there, by rejecting the Lord and refusing to be cleansed of their sins. It's that simple. God wants everyone to come to faith in Him. *Our savior, who wants everyone to be saved and to understand the truth...* (I Timothy 2:3-4)

Only those who reject him will not enter the kingdom. It's their choice, so they are responsible. Jesus has always existed. *Now, Father, bring me into the glory we shared before the world began.* (John 17:5)

I'm fortunate that I work as an end-of-life nurse. Most days, I walk with one foot on this earth and the other touching over into Eternity. It keeps my focus on higher things, rather than the minor issues of this life, most of the time.

If each person who reads this book learns just one thing that improves their relationship or their life, then it was worth the effort! If someone besides me and my friends and family finds my stories funny, even better.

If, after reading these verses, you become curious and start to search for a higher meaning to life than yourself and find Christ as a result, the rewards you'll experience are so great, you can't even imagine the contentment you'll feel. *In the same way, there is more joy in heaven over one sinner who repents and returns to God than over ninety-nine who are righteous and haven't strayed away.* (Luke 15:7)

As the thief who was hanging on a cross next to Jesus said to the other thief, *"Don't you fear God even when you have been sentenced to die? We deserve to die for our crimes, but this man hasn't done anything wrong."* Then he said, *"Jesus, remember me when you come into your kingdom."* And Jesus replied, *"I assure you, today you will be with me in Paradise."* (Luke 23:40-43)

It only takes a second to take this step.

Pray to the Lord and ask for forgiveness for your sins. Accept the free gift that Christ gave you on the cross when he paid for your sins with His life. Say that ten-second prayer to the Lord and become a sealed child of God. Have all of your past, present and future sins erased. This is available to anyone. It's your decision where you'll spend Eternity.

The Lord, my husband and I want you **all** there with us!

Special thanks to our pastor of 22 years, Dan Coggins, who has continually taught us solid truths instead of ear-tickling fluff.

All our thanks to our Lord, who kept waking me up in the middle of the night during my deep sleep and saying, *"Get up and write all you know about marriage."* I had never thought of writing anything before.

Lord, let your will be done!

www.ingramcontent.com/pod-product-compliance
Lightning Source LLC
Chambersburg PA
CBHW051826040426
42447CB00006B/388